ORGANIZATIONAL TEAMWORK
IN HIGH-SPEED MANAGEMENT

SUNY Series, Human Communication Process
Donald P. Cushman and Ted J. Smith, III, Editors

ORGANIZATIONAL TEAMWORK IN HIGH-SPEED MANAGEMENT

YANAN JU
and
DONALD P. CUSHMAN

State University
of New York
Press

Published by
State University of New York Press, Albany

© 1995 State University of New York

All rights reserved

Printed in the United States of America

No part of this book may be used or reproduced
in any manner whatsoever without written permission
except in the case of brief quotations embodied in
critical articles and reviews.

For information, address State University of New York Press,
State University Plaza, Albany, N.Y., 12246

Production by Susan Geraghty
Marketing by Nancy Farrell

Library of Congress Cataloging-in-Publication Data

Chü, Yen-an.
 Organizational teamwork in high-speed management / Yanan Ju and
Donald P. Cushman.
  p. cm. — (SUNY series, human communication processes)
 Includes bibliographical references and index.
  ISBN 0-7914-2237-2 (hc : acid-free). — ISBN 0-7914-2238-0 (pbk. :
acid-free)
  1. Communication in organizations. 2. Communication in
management. 3. Work groups. I. Cushman, Donald P. II. Title.
III. Series: SUNY series in human communication processes.
HD30.3.C48 1995
658.4'036—dc20   94-814
                                                                CIP

10 9 8 7 6 5 4 3 2 1

*This book is dedicated to
Dr. Gavro Altman,
a scholar,
a former ambassador,
a fighter for human dignity,
and a great mutual friend.*

CONTENTS

Preface		ix
Chapter 1	The Promise and Limits of Organizational Teamwork	1
Chapter 2	High-speed Management as a Communication-Based Strategy for Focusing Teamwork on Increasing Competitiveness	11
Chapter 3	Speed-to-Market and International Benchmarking: Teamwork as a Goal-Oriented Action	35
Chapter 4	Defining Qualities and Dominant Patterns of Teamwork	57
Chapter 5	Organizational Structure: A Killer or Facilitator of Teamwork	85
Chapter 6	Team Anchorage in Organizational Life	101
Chapter 7	A Negotiated Linking Program: Communication Strategies for Coaligning an Organization's Internal and External Resources with Its Competitive Environment	115
Chapter 8	Looking into Tomorrow	133
References		139
Index		149

PREFACE

Teamwork for some reason has become a word everyone uses in mission statements, at management seminars, or on an occasion when new organizational visions are hotly debated. Good teamwork practice is nevertheless a rarity. Good teamwork research is even harder to find.

High-speed management sounds interesting but unfamiliar. Few business leaders or managers or organizational researchers have ever heard of the term. Research into it—we mean informed, groundbreaking research—has been close to nonexistent, even though it's on the way.

Putting teamwork and high-speed management together is like walking into a fire without wearing fireproof clothes: one risks coming out burned. We know the stakes involved: putting together two largely unexplored areas requires a lot of conceptual self-struggle and consistency searching on the part of the authors as well as difficult sense making and meaning recreating on the part of our readers. We hope we have not created too many headaches for our readers or for ourselves. We want the text to be reader friendly, so we have worked hard to make it succinct and clear. Throughout our academic life, we have been more readers than authors. We hate jargon and linguistic game playing as much as our readers do.

As far as our reading experiences go, reading a book may not necessarily start from chapter 1 and then continue through chapters 2 and 3 and 4 and 5 and so on until the very end. Watching a movie in a movie theater has to be that way unless you close your eyes. But even if you close your eyes, the most you can do is to avoid seeing something; you can't jump from the end to the middle or the beginning. Reading a book can be more flexible in a sense. You may well start from chapter 2 or any other chapter, particularly when each chapter has been written in such a way that it stands on its own. This is exactly the way we have treated our eight chapters: while there is an easy-to-follow logic in their sequencing, each maintains its own independence.

Indeed the best way to start reading this book, assuming you have limited knowledge of both teamwork and high-speed management, is to start from either chapter 1, which is on teamwork, or chapter 2, which gives more background about high-speed management. And the best time to ask questions is after you have finished both. Readers will have absolutely no problem starting from even the last chapter.

The key to grasping the theme of this book is to keep in mind that both teamwork and high-speed management are conceptualized as *communication processes*; this gives us a common philosophical ground on which we have been allowed to establish linkage between the two at some key dimensions. To put the two processes together, we define teamwork in high-speed management as an organization's or its members' effort to use information and communication to forge an appropriate value-added configuration and linkage among units or otherwise unrelated individual organization members so that the organization is able to respond to the market environment with speed and efficiency and sustain its competitive advantage.

Two other features of this book deserve some attention here. One is that we treat the intersection of organizational teamwork and high-speed management at three different levels: philosophical level, theoretical level, and practical level. Philosophically, modern organizational life is viewed as a dynamic process in which information and communication are used to coalign precious resources to manage a multiplicity of external as well as internal interdependencies. Theoretically, when a specified number of conditions are satisfied, teamwork in a high-speed management context as a set of workable fundamental communication assumptions can generate organizational synergism that will raise the response of an organization to its environment to a high-speed management level. Practically, teamwork as a set of workable fundamental communication assumptions can translate into useful tools and skills for use by all organizations' members, managers and front-line workers alike.

The other feature is that from the very beginning to the very end of the book, we have warned our readers of the limits and possible negative consequences of applying teamwork in a high-speed management context. Teamwork has never been a panacea, and it should never be one. Teamwork, because of its inherent communicative and processual nature, is an open system and, as such, is vulnerable to human misuse or even abuse. The best way to avoid misuse and abuse is to use it appropriately and expertly. And the book is our effort to help, hopefully.

Portions of this book have been presented at national and international conferences or seminars and have appeared in other books either as a chapter or part of a chapter. The figures in this book have been designed with the help of Yifei Ju.

CHAPTER 1

The Promise and Limits of Organizational Teamwork

> Nothing is clearer than the fact that we now live in a rapidly altering, fast moving, hyper-complex world that is too much for a single individual to track, understand and deal with unaided.... Survivors in this turbulent epoch are finding that teamwork and cooperation ignite and fuel the engines of the individual and the enterprise, and make a new level of competency possible.
>
> F. D. Barrett, "Teamwork"

In the 1990s teamwork has become one of an organization's most important activities for achieving excellence in performance (Barrett 1987; Hoerr 1989; Feder 1993). Teamwork has been demonstrated to be central to generating excellence in organizational productivity (Feder 1993), product quality (Hoerr 1989), responsiveness to customer needs (Schroeder and Robinson 1991), and increased sales and profits (Noj 1993). Teamwork is primarily a communication activity (Kelley 1989). Teams are formed in communication and teams achieve excellence in performance only when they excel in their communication (Cushman 1993).

However, recent studies conducted by universities, consulting firms, and organizational training divisions in Europe, Asia, and the United States have found that between 55 percent and 80 percent of all organizational teamwork efforts fail to achieve their organizational goals (*Economist*, Apr. 18, 1992, p. 68; Port et al. 1992, p. 68). These same studies also indicate that when *(a)* organizational teamwork is appropriately guided by a theory of competitive strategy, *(b)* the members of a team are appropriately selected and trained, and *(c)* the team has the support of top man-

---

Portions of this chapter were presented at the Corporate Communication Conference held at Fairleigh Dickinson University in May 1993 under the title When Is Teamwork a Good or When Is It a Bad Solution to Organizational Problems and published in the conference proceedings.

agement, teamwork has been demonstrated to be the primary resource in making a firm a world-class competitor. *It will be the purpose of this book to provide students of the teamwork process with just such a competitive theory, knowledge of the training and skills development process, and means for gaining top management support.*

Prior to entering into the main body of our analysis, we will in this chapter explore what teamwork is and when it is a good and when it is a poor solution to organizational problems. We will then be in a position to provide a broad outline of the remainder of our book.

WHAT IS ORGANIZATIONAL TEAMWORK AND WHEN SHOULD IT BE USED?

> When there is collaboration, when there is coordination, when there is communication, then there is integration, then there is unity, then there is direction and the concentration of energy and talent on the objective. There is enormous force focused upon the task whenever and wherever the magic of integrated effort is manifest.
>
> F. D. Barrett, "Teamwork"

What Are Teamwork's Defining Features?

For a strong sense of corporate teamwork to become operational requires the presence of several specific attitudes and behaviors. *First*, a team must have a common focus, direction, or goal. What makes the focus, direction, or goal of a team unique is the presence in the mind of each team member of a *mutually constructed and publicly agreed to or shared goal*. It is this collaborative effort in establishing and publicly committing to a shared goal in front of one's coworkers that separates a mere collection of individuals or group from a collaborative team (Barrett 1987, p. 24).

Second, a team's performance is constrained, channeled, and focused by a concern for the *appropriate integration of all the team's components* in goal attainment. Corporate team components normally include R&D, manufacturing, marketing, sales, and service functions. When the unique interests, concerns, and contributions of each team component are clearly articulated, collectively understood, and appropriately integrated, the "team's creativity, energy and focus ignites, fueling the engines of the individual and the firm making a new level of competitiveness, quality and performance possible" (Barrett 1987, p. 24).

Third, when coworkers collaborate to form a mutually constructed and publicly committed to goal whose attainment is channeled and constrained by an appropriate integration of the interests, concerns, and contributions of all team members, then they manifest a specific set of behaviors such as mutual respect, trust, and confidence that are unique to effective teamwork and create a *team synergy*. Such collaboration guided by respect, trust, and confidence generates a level of creativity, energy, and integration that produces a focused force more powerful than the sum total of the individual contributions. A team's creativity, energy, and integration is multiplicative, not merely additive (Barrett 1987, p. 24).

The presence of all three of these factors is individually necessary and collectively sufficient to yield teamwork. The absence of any one factor causes teamwork to lapse into mere group effort.

How and Where Is Teamwork Normally Employed in Organizational Functioning?

Some of the most common organizational uses for teamwork involve continuous improvement programs, collective efforts aimed at improving an organization's productivity, product quality, and response time. Within this context, at least five types of teamwork activities can be observed: problem solving, coordination, learning, linking, and decision making. In each case, these activities require teamwork only under the unique circumstance discussed above.

When a unit or organization is confronted with a common problem that requires a joint solution, one everyone can employ with equal agility, then *self-managed teams* are normally employed to *solve the problem*.

When several units in an organization require improved coordination in order to integrate diverse interests, concerns, and contributions to a common goal, then *cross-functional teams* are normally employed to achieve this *increased coordination and integration*.

When a unit or several units in an organization need to master an unusually productive business process employed by another world class organization, then *benchmarking teams* are normally formed to *master this learning process.*

When a unit or organization finds it necessary to control its outsourcing with suppliers, form a joint venture with another firm, or form an alliance with several other firms in order to meet organizational goals, then *outside linking teams* are formed to *negotiate, operationalize, and monitor these liking processes.*

Finally, when upper-level management must make a decision that will influence the entire functioning of an organization, then *executive teams* are set up to *investigate and decide whether and how they should operationalize and implement that decision.*

Self-managed, cross-functional, benchmarking, linking, and executive teamwork have in the past been and will in the future be employed in an attempt to enhance organizational functioning. Unfortunately, recent research suggests that more frequently than not such efforts have failed and may continue to fail if certain conditions are not met. We must therefore explore carefully why this has been and will be so.

What Does Research Tell Us about the Appropriate and Inappropriate Use of Teamwork within an Organizational Work Unit?

First, several studies conducted by consulting firms providing training in the various forms of teamwork involved in continuous improvement programs have found to their dismay that more often than not such forms of teamwork fail to accomplish their goals. Arthur Little in 1991 surveyed five hundred firms involved in their teamwork and continuous improvement training programs and found that only one-third of the firms surveyed felt that their programs were having a significant impact on their competitiveness (*Economist*, Apr. 18, 1992, p. 68). A. T. Kearney surveyed more than one hundred British firms in 1991 and found that only 20 percent believed their teamwork and continuous improvement programs had achieved "tangible results" (p. 68). McKinsey's surveyed sixty firms who had undertaken at least two years of serious efforts at employing teamwork programs and found that most had ground to a halt with the firms reporting that continuation was not worth the cost and effort involved (Port et al. 1992, p. 68). Finally, Rath and Strong asked ninety-five firms to analyze whether "TQM efforts had met such goals as raising market shares or increasing customer satisfaction." They obtained positive evaluations from 26 percent of the firms surveyed (p. 68).

If so many firms that provide training in teamwork and continuous improvement programs are finding the majority of their clients dissatisfied, what can we learn from the research of these programs regarding the appropriate and inappropriate use of teamwork in their organizational context?

Three separate findings shed considerable light on the appropriate and inappropriate use of teamwork: team embeddedness, or anchorage (a term we will use later in the book), leader-team interface, and overall organizational competency. Let's explore each in turn.

The concept of 'embeddedness', or 'anchorage', emerges as the most distinctive feature of teams within large collectivities. Work team development within an organizational context is significantly influenced by the types of team embeddedness in the organization. Four types of connectedness appear particularly important. *First*, there is *task embeddedness* (Cohen and Zhan 1969) *or structural anchorage*, as we will later call it. What type of task has the team been given (learning task, problem-solving task, integration task, performance task, etc.), and what is to be done with the results of the team effort? *Second*, there is *social embeddedness or anchorage*, the relation between the team and its connectedness with the organization's cultural system. What corporate values and climate variables impact the team's developmental process? *Third*, there is *psychological embeddedness or anchorage*, which focuses on how the individual personalities of team members interface (Cohen and Zahn 1969). Teams are made up of individuals with unique interests and interaction styles. These interests and interaction styles significantly influence the development of team processes. *Fourth*, there is *skills embeddedness or anchorage*. What kinds of skills are a team member required to master and how do such skills affect interaction among team members and performance of tasks, particularly in an high-speed management environment?

Where team embeddedness or anchorage intersects the teamwork in such a manner as to prevent the team from (1) developing mutually constructed and publicly agreed to or shared goals, from (2) appropriately integrating the team's members by addressing their unique interests, concerns, and contributions to that shared goal, and/or from (3) generating such behaviors as mutual respect, trust, and confidence that further lead to team synergy, then the task, social, psychological, and skills embeddedness or anchorage will lead to inappropriate teamwork activities.

The interface between an organization's or team's leadership and effective teamwork is equally important. Fiorelli (1988, p. 1), in a study of nineteen teams within an organizational context found that the personality of the team leaders was the chief determinant of team members' behaviors. Lefton and Buzzotta (1987–88) supported and extended Putnam and Fiorelli's analysis in their study of twenty-six top-level management teams operating in large corporations. They found that teamwork was most significantly influenced by the team's interface with the organizational leader's interaction style. The diverse patterns of work groups were found to be a straightforward function of the types of interface found in the group leader. They isolated four distinct patterns and established the frequency with which each occurred in large organizations.

First, there was *a hierarchical pattern* in which groups had strict procedures for the downward transmission of instructions and downward control of outcomes. The leader preferred after an initial meeting to interact with team members singly. The group tasks were divided up and assignments made to each member, who then reported directly to the leader. Group members were encouraged to be positive, not critical, and to ratify the leader's conclusions. "Group members work together not to generate new and better ideas but to implement the leader's ideas" (p. 8). *This pattern of group work occurred in 33 percent of the teams studied.*

Second, there was a *formalistic pattern* in which the group leaders utilized a bureaucratic style of interaction. Here the leader discouraged collaboration to limit unforeseeable consequences. After an initial meeting, members were assigned individual tasks and told to do them the way the organization always does them taking care not to rock the boat. Here the leader believes that "genuine collaboration can be disruptive. Intellectual sparks, once ignited, can kindle anything from a small fire to devastation. A formalist leader avoids this risk by dousing the spark" (p. 9). *This pattern of group work occurs in about 19 percent of the teams studied.*

Third, there is a *circular pattern* in which group leaders insisted on collaboration, comraderie, and collegiality in dealing with group members but not in dealing with the team task. This pattern dominated whenever harmony and equality were the key group values. Compromise and appeasement took the place of the open and critical evaluation of the problem. "The circular pattern is almost always present whenever the leader of a group says things like: 'around here, we're all one big happy family' and 'we are people who get along with one another'" (p. 9). *This form of group work occurred in 9 percent of the cases under study.*

Fourth, there was the genuine *teamwork pattern* in which leaders encouraged the development and attainment of a mutually constructed, publicly agreed to, and shared goal whose attainment was channeled and constrained by an appropriate concern for the integration of all the team's components, thus manifesting mutual respect, trust, and confidence in the teamwork process. Leaders, while remaining in charge, encouraged the team to set goals, do planning, and implement actions that would serve the entire team's needs.

What distinguished this teamwork pattern from others was the prevalence of candid and committed interplay. The candor was evident in the ease and frankness that marked discussions; team members argued and disagreed without embarrassment or discomfort. In place of the zestful malice so often seen among adversaries, there was constructive openness of partners. The commitment was evident in the degree of involvement; each member believed that the work of the team is important and that he or she could affect the outcome. As a result, the team went about its work with spirited seriousness. A high degree of synergism usually resulted (p. 9). *This pattern occurred in about 40 percent of the instances under investigation.*

The patterns of communication behaviors characteristic of each sequence as reported by participants on a five-point scale are listed in table 1.1.

Each of the above patterns of group work occurs within all organizations. Each has its own outcomes and organizational leadership style. The important thing for organizational leaders to understand is how to match a team's leadership style to the preferred team outcomes. The important thing for team members to realize is which type of leader a team has and thus what are considered productive communication activities for team members under each style.

Finally, an organization's overall performance as an indicator of its general knowledge and competence level is as important as team embeddedness or anchorage and the leadership-team interface. Ernst and Young in 1992 examined 584 firms employing

TABLE 1.1
Self-Assessment of the Top-Level Teams in Ten Activities

	Hierarchical	Formalistic	Circular	Teamwork	Totals
Coordination within team	4.3	1.9	0.4	3.4	10.0
Profitability/ Cost awareness	3.9	1.6	1.0	3.5	10.0
Communications	3.7	2.2	1.2	2.9	10.0
Conflict/ Disagreement	3.3	2.3	1.3	3.1	10.0
Meetings	4.0	1.4	0.7	3.9	10.0
Organization/ Control	3.3	1.4	0.7	4.6	10.0
Decision making/ Problem solving	2.9	2.4	0.7	4.0	10.0
Goal setting/ Planning	2.9	1.4	0.7	5.0	10.0
Coordination with other units	2.3	2.0	1.1	4.6	10.0
Critique and feedback	2.4	2.7	1.0	3.9	10.0
Total	3.3	1.9	0.9	3.9	10.0

teamwork in their continuous improvement programs and found a strong correlation between the successful use of different types of teamwork and the overall competency levels of an organization as reflected in general profitability and productivity levels (Port et al. 1992, pp. 66–67).

More specifically, the Ernst and Young study found that if a firm had a return on assets (ROA) of less than 2 percent and a value added per employee (VAE) of less than $47,000, they should follow the position of the model for *novices*. If a firm had an ROA of 2 percent to 6.9 percent and a VAE of $47,000 to $73,999, then they should follow the pattern for *journeyman*. If a firm had an ROA of 7 percent or higher and a VAE of $74,000 and up, they should follow the pattern for *master* firms.

When a firm's overall organizational performance has been determined, then the tasks and types of teamwork they can effectively learn how to employ are set by the firm's overall organizational competence.

In conclusion, this is when and where teamwork will or will not work:

1. When a firm's task, social, psychological, and skills embeddedness or anchorage allows teamwork to develop mutually constructed and publicly agreed to goals and/or appropriately integrating each team member's unique interests, concerns, and contributions, then teamwork should be employed. Otherwise, it will not work.
2. When the leadership of a firm provides an appropriate team leader interface with a team, then teamwork should be employed. Without such a leader-team interface, there will be no teamwork.
3. When the overall performance of a firm has been appropriately assessed, then only that form of teamwork appropriate to its general level of competence should be employed. Other forms will have less or no chance to succeed.

AN OVERVIEW FOR THE REMAINDER OF THE BOOK

> What distinguishes the teamwork pattern is the prevalence of candid and committed interplay. The candor is evident in the easy frankness that marks discussion; team members argue and disagree without embarrassment or discomfiture. In place of the zestful malice so often seen among adversaries, there's the constructive openness of partners. The commitment is evident in the degree of involvement, each member believes that the work of the team is important and that he or she can affect the outcome. As a result, the team goes about its work with spiritual seriousness. A high degree of synergism usually results.
>
> R. Lefton and V. R. Buzzotta, "Teams and Teamwork"

The remainder of the book will discuss various teamwork processes and components that combine to generate this "high degree of synergism" that high-speed management organizations would need to create competitive advantage. We wish to remind our readers, before they read on, what sets this book apart from others in the field is our effort to identify a connection between teamwork and high-speed management, or rather, pinpoint some of the special characteristics of organizational teamwork in the context of high-speed management.

Chapter 2 discusses high-speed management as a communication-based framework of competitive strategy within which we will take a new look at organizational teamwork. The focus of the discussion will be on environmental scanning and value chain theory.

Chapter 3 probes speed-to-market as a primary teamwork goal and international benchmarking as a way to achieving that goal.

Chapter 4 explores defining qualities and dominant patterns of organizational teamwork in the context of high-speed management and their exemplary applications at two of the world's best performing organizations, Toyota Motor Company in Japan and General Electric in the United States A model of teamwork in the framework of high-speed management is presented toward the end of the chapter.

Chapter 5 examines organizational structure as a killer or facilitator of teamwork in organizations following high-speed management principles.

Chapter 6 takes a look at team embeddedness or anchorage in organizational life, again, from a high-speed management perspective.

Chapter 7 looks at a negotiated linking program as a paradigm teamwork strategy for coaligning an organization's internal and external resources with its competitive environment.

Chapter 8 outlines present accomplishments and future prospects for teamwork within a high-speed management framework.

CHAPTER 2

High-Speed Management as a Communication-Based Strategy for Focusing Teamwork on Increasing Competitiveness

> There is currently a convergence of attention and concern among managers and management scholars across the basic issues of organizational success and failure.... Successful organizations achieve strategic fit with their environment and support their strategies with appropriately designed structures and management processes, less successful organizations typically exhibit poor fit externally and/or internally.
>
> R. Miles and C. Snow, "Fit, Failure, and the Hall of Fame"

Regardless of which corporations or nations emerge as leaders in the high-technology race, the world high-technology market has given rise to a new system of management that is revolutionizing the way work gets done. This new *high-speed management system* is a set of principles, strategies, and tools for coming up with a steady flow of new products, making sure they are what the customer wants, designing and manufacturing them with speed and precision, getting them to the market quickly, and servicing them easily in order to make large profits and satisfy consumer needs (Pepper 1989). High-speed management, which began in the high-technology sector, is now diffusing, with promising results,

---

This chapter has been published and reprinted in several sources: High-Speed Management: A Revolution in Organizational Communication the 1990s (with S. King); in M. Cross and W. Cummins, eds., The Proceedings of the Fifth Conference on Corporate Communication, Fairleigh Dickinson University, Madison, N.J., 1992, pp. 99–123. Reprinted in Stanley Deetz, ed., Communication Yearbook 16 (1993), pp. 209–37; in S. King and D. P. Cushman, eds., High-Speed Management and Organizational Communication in the 1990s: A Reader (Albany: SUNY Press, 1994), pp. 5–40; in M. Goodman, ed, Corporate Communication: Theory and Practice (Albany: SUNY Press, in press).

to all public, private, and nonprofit sectors of the world economy (Stalk 1988). High-speed management systems have at their core a new conceptualization of the role information and communication must play in organizational functioning, a role that generates a unique form of sustainable competitive advantage and is grounded in a new set of principles, strategies, and techniques of organizational communication (Cushman and King 1993b).

Our purpose in this section is to provide a broad outline of the theory of high-speed management and of the principles, strategies, and techniques that undergird its effectiveness and to demonstrate their implications for teamwork as a communication process impacting a firm's competitiveness. In so doing, we will (1) briefly explore the convergence of four trends that have led to the emergence of high-speed management, (2) outline the general theory of high-speed management, and (3) examine some of the transformations high-speed management has brought about in the traditional conceptualization of organizational teamwork communication processes.

FOUR TRENDS THAT HAVE LED TO THE EMERGENCE OF HIGH-SPEED MANAGEMENT

Prior to entering into the main body of our analysis, we shall explore four trends, the convergence of which has led to the restructuring of the global economic environment, placing new demands on corporate management and giving rise to high-speed management systems:

1. Several breakthroughs have taken place in information and communication technologies that have dramatically changed how organizational manufacturing, marketing, and management work.
2. This information and communication revolution has helped facilitate a dramatic increase in world trade, the emergence of a global economy, and the development of three large core markets.
3. These technological breakthroughs and increases in world trade have created a volatile business climate characterized by rapidly changing technology, quick market saturation,

and unexpected competition, making success in business difficult to achieve.
4. To compete successfully in such an environment, executives must employ management theories and practices that emphasize innovation, adaptation, flexibility, efficiency, and rapid response.

We will elaborate on each of these trends briefly.

Breakthroughs in Information and Communication Technologies

Several technological breakthroughs have taken place that make possible the generation, processing, and instant delivery of information and communication throughout the world, creating a revolution in organizational manufacturing, marketing, and management. At the center of this revolution is a constellation of new management tools based on computers and telecommunications. Taken collectively, these tools provide a new way of thinking and acting in regard to all the problems that confront management in dealing with a rapidly changing economic environment.

New Manufacturing technologies employ computer-aided and telecommunication-linked engineering, manufacturing, and resource planning processes to allow for the rapid development, production, sales, and service of customerized new products at low cost, high quality, and easy service throughout the world (Young 1990). Allen-Bradley, a Milwaukee manufacturer of industrial controls, possesses one of the world's most modern computer-aided and telecommunication-linked engineering, manufacturing, and resource planning facilities. This facility can produce one of a product or one hundred thousand of the same product at the same per unit cost. This plant can receive the specifications for an order one day and deliver the product to its destination the next, cutting the average turnaround time on orders from four weeks to two days. Under this system, engineering and manufacturing costs have decreased 40 percent at the same time profits have increased by 32 percent and product quality has increased by 200 percent (Port 1986).

New marketing information technologies employ computer-aided and telecommunication-linked environmental scanning, electronic test marketing, and real-time merchandising for speed in providing customers with world-class products when and where whey want them in order to increase market shares (Young 1990). Campbell Soup Company, for example, can scan the environment to determine customer desire for a new soup, then computer model its contents; simulate its production; calibrate its cost, price, profits, and sales potential; develop an artificial intelligence system to control its rate and quality of production; pretest its name, taste, shelf placement, and type and content of its advertising; and run its test markets—reducing a management decision-making process that used to take years to a matter of two or three days. These new marketing technologies cut the cost of this process by 30 percent while increasing product success rates by 80 percent (Russell, Adams, and Boundy 1986).

New management information technologies employ computer-aided and telecommunication-linked decision support, operational research, artificial intelligence, and group technology systems to integrate, coordinate, and control management processes in order to create competitive advantage. American Express has implemented an artificial intelligence system that provides decision support for managers making authorization decisions on individual purchases from four hundred thousand shops and restaurants throughout the world. This expert system has reduced by 20 percent the turnaround time per transaction and has reduced by 50 percent the number of authorizations in trouble ninety days after approval, while providing annual savings of $27 million (Feigenbaum, McCorduck, and Nii 1988).

New manufacturing, marketing, and management information technologies, when appropriately employed, allow for more effective integration, coordination, and control of all organizational processes, creating the potential for competitive advantage (Young 1990). These are some of the new information and communication tools that, when taken collectively, are creating a new way of thinking and acting in regard to the interests of managers, stockholders, workers, customers, and competitors throughout major portions of the globe. Similarly, such world-class information and communication capability allows organizations to track and respond in real time to international changes in the cost of capital, labor, raw materials, consumer taste, and competitor response.

Increased World Trade

The ability of corporations to track in real time the needs of customers and changes in the cost of capital, labor, and raw materials throughout the world has led to *(a)* a rapid increase in world trade, *(b)* the emergence of a global economy, and *(c)* strong regional markets. Driven by information and communication technologies and the competitive advantages they create, world trade over the past four decades has grown much faster than the world's gross world GNP. International exports and imports were about one-fifth the world GNP in 1962, one-fourth in 1972, one-third in 1982, and are projected to approach one-half the world GNP in 1992 ("Global Giants" 1990).

Over the past decade, a single model of economic development has emerged that is influencing economic policies throughout the nations involved in the emerging global economy. The generalization of such a model should not be taken to imply that all governments or all economies are alike; it merely suggests broad central tendencies in the economic policies of most nations as they begin to participate in the global economy. This model includes seven general features:

1. control of inflation through fiscal austerity and monetary restrictions
2. reduction of labor costs as a percentage of product costs
3. increasing productivity and profitability through the effective use of information and communication technology
4. restructuring of industrial and service sectors by disinvesting from low-profit areas and investing in high-growth, high-profit areas
5. privatization and deregulation of some aspects of the economy by withdrawing from state ownership and control in favor of open market forces
6. relative control over the pricing of raw materials and energy, assuring the stability of pricing systems and exchange flows
7. opening up gradually to world markets and increased internationalization of economies

As Castells (1986) argues:

Such a model is not necessarily linked to a particular political party or administration, or even to a country, even though the Reagan or Thatcher governments seem to be the closest examples of the fulfillment of these policies. But very similar policies have developed in most West European countries, in those governed by Socialists, and even in Communist-led regions (Italy) or Communist-participating governments (France, for a certain period). At the same time, in most Third World countries, austerity policies, inspired or dictated by the International Monetary Fund and world financial institutions, have also developed along the same line, establishing not without contradictions and conflicts (Walton 1985) a new economic logic that is not only capitalistic but a very specific kind of capitalism. (p. 300)

With the emerging global economy, competitive advantage is shifting toward those regions of the world with *(a)* large core markets, *(b)* strong scientific and technological work forces, and *(c)* private and public economic sectors that can attract the capital necessary to provide the infrastructure needed for increased growth and technological changes. The U.S./Canadian core market, the European Community core market, and the Japanese area of influence in Asia appear to meet these criteria (Baig 1989).

The Volatile Business Climate

Rapidly changing technology, quick market saturation, unexpected global competition—these all make succeeding in business, particularly a high-technology business, harder than ever today (Fraker 1984). The volatile business climate engendered by the information technology and communication revolution and the globalization of economic forces has led to a significant realignment of individual corporate resources. In order to contribute to an understanding of this corporate realignment, we will explore the unique problem this realignment creates for individual corporations and outline the new corporate perspective for responding to this problem.

Most of the environmental forces precipitating the need for rapid change in corporate operations arise from a single problem—the fact that firms are confronted by *shrinking product life cycles*. The product life cycle is the period of the time available from the inception of an idea for a product until the market for that product is saturated or disappears due to new product development. A product life cycle normally involves several stages: conceptualization, design, testing, refinement, mass production, marketing, shipping, selling, and servicing. Dominique Hanssens, a professor at UCLA's Graduate School of Management, has studied the product life cycle in electrical appliances for years. He reports that years ago the product life cycle for refrigerators took more than thirty years to mature, providing considerable time for each phase to develop (cited in Fraker 1984). However, all of this has changed. The market for microwave ovens has taken ten years to mature; for CB radios, four years; for computer games, three years; and so on. Perhaps the most dramatic example of shrinking product life cycle as result of rapidly changing technology, quick market saturation, and unexpected competition can be found in the computer industry (Berlant, Browning, and Foster 1990).

The first commercially successful computer, containing an eight-bit memory chip, came to market in 1977; four years later, in 1981, the sixteen-bit memory chip appeared; in 1983 came the thirty-two-bit memory chip; and in 1984 came the sixty-four-bit memory chip. By 1987, we witnessed the appearance of the one-megabyte memory chip, by 1989 the four-megabyte memory chip, and by 1990 the development of a sixteen-megabyte memory chip was well under way. The industrial shakedown from such rapid changes has taken its toll. Large U.S. companies once dominant in their respective markets, such as Hewlett-Packard, Apple, and DEC, who were unable to respond effectively to the end of one product life cycle and the beginning of a new one, lost their market position, with still other firms going out the computer business.

How can a company manage to avoid these unpleasantries and prosper? What new techniques and skills must managers master to respond to this challenge? Only recently have executives who have responded successfully to this challenge begun to report a consistent pattern of attack that shows promise of providing a foundation for a new corporate perspective on how to respond to rapid environmental change.

Fraker (1984) argues that a rapidly changing technology, quick market saturation, and unexpected competition have led to the emergence of a new corporate perspective for coping with a volatile business climate. The following seven elements together form the basis of a new set of corporate assumptions and practices:

1. *Companies must stay close to both their customers and their competitors.* Successful companies always know what the customer needs and attempt to provide it. When products and manufacturing processes change rapidly, it is crucial to keep up with the investment strategies and product costs of rival companies. In order to accomplish this, companies must develop and maintain a rapid and accurate intelligence system capable of preventing surprises.

2. *Companies must think constantly about new products and then back that thinking with quick investment.* A good new product strategy requires a large, active, and focused research and development team with ready access to and the prudent use of large amounts of capital.

3. *Rapid and effective delivery requires close coordination among design, manufacturing, testing, marketing, delivery, and servicing systems.* The interdependence of these systems, combined with the short lead time in product delivery, makes certain that any error within or between systems will delay product delivery and endanger market penetration. Close cooperation among systems requires strong, quick, and responsive integration, coordination, and control.

4. *Product quality, user friendliness, ease of service, and competitive pricing are essential for market penetration.* In an environment where consumer and investor representatives compare, rate, and effectively communicate product differences, market penetration depends on quality, utility, and readily serviceable products. This in turn requires the active monitoring, testing, and checking of service for one's own and competitive products.

5. *Companies that introduce new products must consider the processes and costs required to cannibalize their own products and to retrench the workers involved.* Companies faced with rapidly changing technology, quick market saturation, and unexpected competition must be prepared to change or withdraw their own products rather than let their reputations and market shares be eroded by competitors. Corporate planning for new products must include contingencies for shifting, retraining, or retrenching large product sectors rapidly.

6. *A corporate vision must be developed that emphasizes change, allows for the assimilation of new units with alternative values, and encourages members to learn from mistakes without reprisal.* Corporate cultures that cannot change rapidly will

impede market adaptation. Corporations faced with stiff competition will often acquire other corporations with alternative values that will have to be integrated without delay into their corporate culture. Finally, a certain number of new initiatives are doomed to failure for all the reasons previously cited. Talented members of an organization must learn quickly from their failures and press on to new projects.

7. *A corporate strategy must be developed that scans the globe for potential acquisitions, joint ventures, coalitions, value-added partnerships, and tailored trade agreements that can give a corporation a technological edge, market access, market control, and/or rapid response capabilities.* Such a pooling of corporate resources is necessary for survival in a rapidly changing, highly competitive international economic environment(Cushman and king 1994).

Employment of New Management Assumptions

Rapid environmental change creates organizational problems, but it can also create organizational opportunities. An organization's management system, with its integration, coordination, and control processes, must have certain specifiable characteristics in order to respond to the opportunities created by successive, rapid, environmental change. A management system that capitalizes on environmental change must be *(a)* innovative, *(b)* adaptive, *(c)* flexible, *(d)* efficient, and *(e)* rapid in response—a high-speed management system.

> *Innovative management* refers not only to product development, but to innovation in corporate structure, human resources utilization, outsourcing, inventory control, manufacturing, marketing, servicing, and competitive positioning.
>
> *Adaptive management* refers to an organization's appropriate adjustment to change in employee values, customer tastes, investor interests, government regulations, the availability of global economic resources, and the strategic positioning of competitors.
>
> *Flexible management* refers to the capacity of an organization to expand, contract, and shift direction on products and competitive strategy; to assimilate acquisitions, joint ventures, and

coalitions; and to excise unproductive or underproductive units.

Efficient management refers to maintaining the industry lead in world-class products, productivity, investors' equity, return on investment, employee satisfaction, customer support, product quality, and serviceability.

Rapid response management refers to setting and maintaining the industry standard in speed of response to environmental change.

The organizational benefits that flow from a high-speed management system can be very significant. *First, order-of-magnitude changes occur in response time.* General Electric reduced from three weeks to three days the amount of time required to deliver a custom-made circuit breaker. Motorola used to turn out electronic pagers three weeks after the factory order arrived; now the process takes two hours (Ruffin 1990).

Second, order-of-magnitude changes occur in productivity, product quality, and market shares. A recent survey of fifty major U.S. corporations by Kaiser and Associates, a large consulting firm, found that all listed time-based management strategies at the top of their priority ranking (Dumaine 1989, p. 54). Why? Because speed of response tends to provide order-of-magnitude improvements in productivity, profits, product quality, and market shares.

Third, order-of-magnitude changes occur in profits. McKinsey & Company management consulting group has demonstrated that high-tech products that come to market six months late earn 33 percent less profit over five years than those coming out with a product on time and that 50 percent over budget increase in product development cuts profits only 4 percent when the product is on time (cited in Vesey 1991, p. 25).

The focus of this new corporate perspective, and thus the goal of high-speed management, is the use of the new information technologies and human communication processes to develop, test, and produce rapidly a steady flow of low-cost, high-quality, easily serviced, high-value products that meet the customers' needs and to get these products to market quickly, before the competition, in an effort to achieve market penetration and large profits.

AN OUTLINE OF THE THEORY OF HIGH-SPEED MANAGEMENT

Competitive advantage in a rapidly changing economic environment will depend upon a corporation's capacity to monitor changes in *external economic forces* accurately and then to reorder a firm's *internal resources* rapidly to respond effectively to these external economic forces. In order to monitor changes in external economic forces accurately, an organization must have world-class information and communication capability. Such capability allows an organization to track and to respond in real time to international changes in the costs of capital, labor, and raw materials as well as changes in consumer taste and competitor response.

Similarly, sustainable competitor advantage in the 1990s will depend upon a corporation's capacity to orient and reorient rapidly a firm's product development, purchasing, manufacturing, distribution, sales, and service systems in response to volatile environmental change. To understand and employ a high-speed management system systematically, we are in need of a theoretical framework to guide the development and maintenance of such a world-class information and communication capability. It is the purpose of this portion of our discussion to explicate such a general theoretical framework. Our explication proceeds in two stages. *First*, we explore a theory of environmental scanning as an information and communication framework for monitoring and evaluating rapid changes in an organization's external economic forces. *Second*, we explore value chain theory as an information and communication framework for rapidly orienting and reorienting an organization's internal resources in response to changing external environmental forces. *Third*, we investigate continuous improvement programs as a method for employing teamwork to improve the productivity, quality, and adaptation of the value chain to customer needs.

A Theory of Environmental Scanning

Environments create both problems and opportunities for organizations. Organizations must cope with changes in the costs of capital, labor, and raw materials; with shifts in consumer tastes, government regulations, and political stability; and with unexpected competition. Similarly, organizations depend upon the environment for scarce and valued resources and for development of strategic alliances—such as coalitions, licensing, acquisitions, joint ventures, consortia, value-added partnerships, and tailored trade agreements—aimed at improving R&D, manufacturing, distribution and service, and sales capabilities. An organization's environment, perhaps more than any other factor, affects organizational strategy, structure, and performance. However, whether changes in organizational strategy, structure, and performance lead to positive or negative consequences rests almost entirely upon the speed, accuracy, and interpretation of the information and communication regarding various environmental changes and the rapid reorientation of an organization's strategy, structure, and resource in order to take advantage of such changes. Environmental scanning is explored below in two stages: an explication of an environmental scanning framework and an example of environmental scanning by a high-performance firm.

An Explication of a Theory of Environmental Scanning   If environmental scanning is an essential information and communication process for reorienting organizational strategy, structure, and resources, then how is this monitoring to be achieved? Each industry and market in which a firm operates will contain its own unique underlying dynamic based upon what competitors are doing to influence sales and the influences to which the firm's customers are responding in buying products. Thus environmental scanning of industry and market forces must track the organizational strategies, structures, and resources employed by competitors and the tasks, inclinations, products, and potential products that the firm's own customers will want or demand.

Once the competitive dynamics of an industry and market are understood, top-level managers normally scan the economic, technical, political, and social forces at work in the global economy that might be employed by competitors and/or their own firm to influence these competitive dynamics. For example, capital can frequently be borrowed from Japanese banks at 3 percent to 5 percent less than from other sources; skilled labor can be obtained in Singapore, Taiwan, and Korea at 30 percent to 60 percent less than in the U.S.-Canadian and European Community markets; parts and manufacturing processes can frequently be subcontracted from other firms less expensively than they can be provided in house. These global forces can significantly influence the competitive dynamics of an industry and market and are central to reorienting a firm to achieve a competitive advantage.

Environmental Scanning in a High-Performance Organization
Environmental scanning is at once a simple and a complex process. It is simple in that the critical information required to analyze the underlying dynamics of an industry and market is frequently readily available to all the competitors. It is complex in that the number of areas monitored that affect this dynamic may be large. Let us explore the elements in this process in a concrete example.

Jack Welch, CEO of General Electric (GE), a very successful global competitor, describes the two levels of environmental scanning and their effects on corporate alignment in his firm. Once a year, at the annual meeting of GE's top one hundred executives, each of the firm's thirteen business leaders is required to present an environmental scanning analysis of his or her respective businesses. Each business leader is asked to present one-page answers to five questions:

1. What are your business global market dynamics today and where are they going over the next several years?
2. What actions have your competitors taken in the last three years to upset those global dynamics?
3. What have you done in the last three years to affect those dynamics?
4. What are the most dangerous things your competitors could do in the next three years to upset those dynamics?
5. What are the most effective things you could do to bring about your desired impact on those dynamics?

Welch concludes:

> Five simple charts. After those initial reviews, which we update regularly, we could assume that everyone at the top knew the plays and had the same playbook. It doesn't take a genius. So when Larry Bossidy is with a potential partner in Europe, or I'm with a company in the Far East, we're always there with a competitive understanding based on our playbooks. We know exactly what makes sense; we don't need a big staff to do endless analysis. That means we should be able to act with speed.

Probably the most important thing we promise our business leaders is fast action. Their job is to create and grow new global business. Our job in the executive is to facilitate, to go out and negotiate a deal, to make the acquisition, or get our businesses the partners they need. When our business leaders call, they don't expect studies, they expect answers.

Take the deal with Thomson, where we swapped our consumer electronics business for their medical equipment business. We were presented with an opportunity, a great solution to a serious strategic problem and we were able to act quickly. We didn't need to go back to headquarters for a strategic analysis and a bunch of reports. Conceptually, it took us about 30 minutes to decide that the deal made sense and then maybe two hours with the Thomson people to work out the basic terms. (quoted in Tichy and Charzon 1989, p. 115)

Environmental scanning allows us to focus on the forces external to an organization that significantly influence its internal relationships. Value chain theory allows us the opportunity to reorient an organization's internal relationships in an effort to influence the organization's response to external forces.

Value Chain Theory

We are in need of a theoretical framework for analyzing the kinds of international markets, the types of competitive advantage, and the issues involved in configuring and liking a firm's activities relative to its competitors so as to obtain a sustainable competitive advantage. Particularly useful in this regard is value chain theory. We shall therefore explicate value chain theory, apply this theory to an analysis of competitive advantage in the international auto industry, and draw out the implications of this analysis for high-speed management.

The basic unit of analysis in understanding international competition is the industry, because it is in the industry that market shares are won or lost. In order to analyze how international competition functions, we must explore various market strategies, types of competitive advantage, and how value chain theory can serve as a theoretical approach for developing the sources of competitive advantage within an organization's functioning.

The forms of international competition within an industry range from multidomestic to global. A *multidomestic* approach to markets treats each country or core market as a unique arena and adjusts a firm's strategy for obtaining a competitive advantage to the specific issue in that market. When a firm takes this market-by-market approach, its international strategy is multidomestic. A multidomestic firm views its industry as a collection of individual markets. Such a firm normally operates relatively autonomous subsidiaries in each market.

A *global* approach to markets is one in which a firm's competitive position in one country or core market is significantly affected by that firm's competitive position in other countries or core markets. International competition in a global industry is more than a collection of independent subsidiaries located in individual markets with unique strategies for obtaining competitive advantage in each market. A global approach rests on a series of interdependent activities that are integrated, coordinated, and controlled so that competitive advantage in one part of the world can be leveraged to obtain competitive advantage throughout the linkage system.

Competitive advantage can be viewed conceptually as emanating from four sources:

1. A product or service that provides customers with comparable value at lower cost than offered by competitors creates *low-cost competitive advantage.* Japanese auto makers have consistently produced cars at $750 to $950 per unit lower cost than comparable American manufacturers, leading to low-cost competitive advantage (Treece and Howr 1989, p. 75).

2. A product or service that is comparable in cost but that contains some unique quality, styling, service, or functional features relative to competitor creates *differentiation competitive advantage.* Toyota and Honda automobiles require fewer repairs, are easier to service, and have more standard features (such as air conditioning, power brakes and steering, and AM-FM radios) included in the product price, and they thus create higher customer satisfaction than similar U.S. and European cars and a product differentiation competitive advantage.

3. A broader range of products or services than offered by competitors creates *scope competitive advantage.* The Ford Motor Corporation provides its customers with small, medium, large, luxury, and sports cars and station wagons to select from, as well as a broad range of trucks and minivans, creating competitive advantage relative to the Chrysler Corporation based on product scope.

4. Due to the high demand for certain products or services, the first producer into the market with a quality product can dominate the market and obtain high-end pricing and maximize profits based on speed of response, creating a *time competitive advantage*. The Chrysler Corporation's development, production, and marketing of minivans beat its competitors to market by one year, allowing Chrysler to capture all of the market for minivans for one year and get high-end pricing for maximum profits, and to hold a majority of the market (51 percent) for the next two years due to its time competitive advantage.

Most top international firms seek to exploit competitive advantage from all four sources. To diagnose where the sources of a firm's competitive advantage are and how each organization's functional units and business processes add value or fail to add value to products, we need a theoretical framework for disaggregating a firm's discrete activities and evaluating their value-added contribution to an organization's products. Value chain theory is such a framework. Managers term the discrete activities involved in producing a product or service the "value chain"; they arrange these activities into functional unit activities and business processes (see fig. 2.1).

In examining an organization's *functional unit level* of the value chain, notice that the two circles in the figure that denote suppliers and customers are normally found outside the organizational structure, while the boxes between the circles denote functional activities performed within an organization's structure. In examining an organization's *business process level*, note how each process includes some activities unique to each business process and some activities that overlap with other business processes.

Functional units and business processes may be located anywhere on the globe they can gain competitive advantage from their location. *Product development processes* are normally located in regions where firms have access to a steady supply of state-of-the-art engineers, such as the United States, Japan, and Germany, where competitive advantage can be obtained from product differentiation. *Product delivery processes* are normally located near sources of inexpensive and skilled labor and automated production facilities, such as Korea, Singapore, and Taiwan, where competitive advantage can be obtained from low-cost production. *Customer service and management teams* are nor-

FIGURE 2.1
An Organizations Value Chain

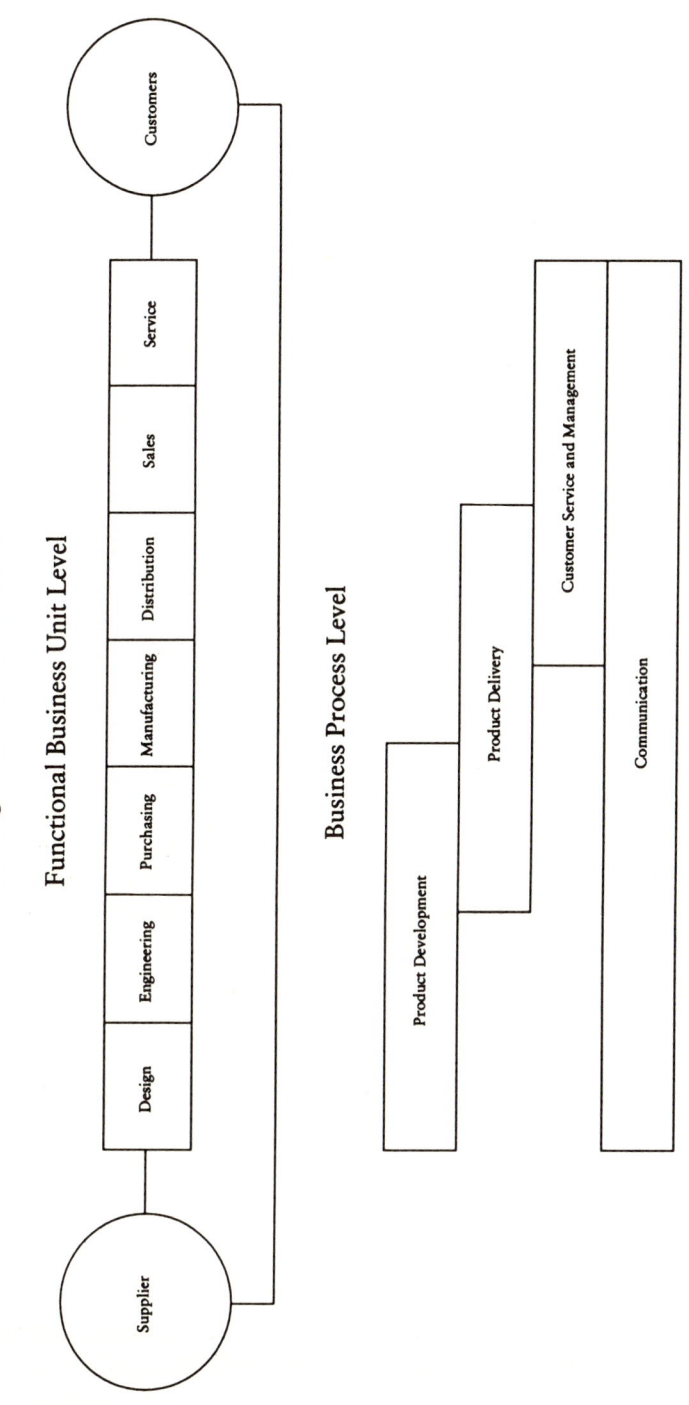

Functional Business Unit Level

Supplier — Design | Engineering | Purchasing | Manufacturing | Distribution | Sales | Service — Customers

Business Process Level

Product Development

Product Delivery

Customer Service and Management

Communication

Source: Adapted from Rockart and Short 1989, p. 12

mally located in the core markets that a firm services in order to obtain competitive advantage from rapid response time. A firm may obtain competitive advantage and/or value-added contribution from one or more of these sources. However, competitive advantage and value-added activities gained in one functional unit or business process can be added to or cancelled out by an organization's performance in other functional units or business processes. This is what is meant by value-added or value-diminishing chains of activities. If a functional unit or business activity fails to provide a source of competitive advantage or to add value to an organization's products, then it needs to be improved or replaced. A primary function of management is to employ information and communication to monitor, evaluate, and improve the value chain in order to gain competitive advantage. This is essentially a communication process. The information and communication component of this process will be explored in detail later in the chapter.

An Application of Value Chain Theory to the Global Auto Industry The international auto market is a multibillion-dollar industry in which ten firms account for approximately 78 percent of the world sales. Table 2.1 provides a profile of the September 1988 to September 1989 global performance of these firms. The top three—General Motors, Ford, and Toyota—account for more than 40 percent of the world auto market. We shall, for reasons of space, limit our analysis to the international competition among the top three firms in the U.S. core market. The central competitive dynamics operating in the global automobile industry, according to Harold Poling (1989), CEO of Ford Motor Corporation, are "vehicle attributions, customer satisfaction and value for money." *Vehicle attributes* refers to styling, power train performance, and road handling. *Customer satisfaction* refers to vehicle comfort, safety, quality, and ease of maintenance. *Value for money* refers to cost, standard features, gas mileage, and insurance costs.

Table 2.2 provides the relevant high-speed management data upon which our analysis for the U.S. market is based. The General Motors Corporation (GM) is the world's largest producer of automobiles. Its U.S. market shares have fallen from 45 percent in 1980 to 35 percent in 1989. A drop of 1 percent amounts to 114,526 cars. GM's market shares at the lower-end auto price

TABLE 2.1
World Auto Market, September 1988–September 1989

	World % of Market Share	Auto Revenues (Billions)	Net Earnings (Thousands)	Worldwide Vehicles (Thousands)	Production Autos (%)	Trucks (%)
GM	17.7	99.7	3,831	7,946	74	26
Ford	14.6	76.8	4,259	6,336	70	30
Toyota	9.4	53.8	2,836	4,115	76	24
Volkswagen	6.6	34.4	921	2,948	93	7
Nissan	6.4	36.4	945	2,930	77	23
Chrysler	5.4	30.8	629	2,382	48	52
Fiat	5.4	26.4	2,453	2,436	90	10
Peugeot	4.6	22.8	1,518	2,216	88	12
Renault	4.2	26.4	1,451	2,053	80	20
Honda	4.0	25.2	945	1,960	86	14

Source: Adapted from Borrus, 1990.

range have been eroded by Ford Escort and Toyota Tercel, at the middle price range by Ford Taurus and Tempo as well as Toyota Corolla, and at the upper price range by Ford Lincoln and Toyota Camry. GM has invested $46 billion in plant modernization (a sum equal to the amount needed to purchase Toyota Motors in 1990) and is still the high-cost producer. GM in the past three years cut $15 billion from its operating budget, closed several plants, and laid off workers but still ran its remaining plants at 70 percent of their capacity, compared with 78 percent and 110 percent for Ford and Toyota, respectively. As the high-speed management data show, GM requires more worker hours per car and more model replacement time, and has had a lower productivity increase than its two competitors. In addition, GM's Cadillac, Oldsmobile, and Buick cars ranked 7, 8, and 9, respectively, in quality ratings, while Toyota's Corolla and Camry ranked two and three; no Ford cars appeared in the top ten (Taylor 1990a).

The Ford Motor Corporation was one of America's most successful global competitors in the 1980s. Ford's market shares increased from 20 percent in 1980 to 22 percent by 1989. Ford produced vehicles at $200 less per unit than GM, but trailed Toyota by $650 per unit in cost. Over the past years Ford has invested $21 billion in plant modernization and has significantly improved its production capabilities. It is evident from our high-speed man-

TABLE 2.2
High-Speed Management Data for the U.S. Market

	GM	Ford	Toyota
Market share, 1980 (%)	45	20	6
Market share, 1989 (%)	35	22	7
Market share, 1990 (%)	35	22	9
Productivity (worker hours per car)	20	17	12
Average replacement time (years per model), 1990	5	5	2
Factory utilization of capacity available, 1990 (%)	70	78	110
Productivity Increase, 1990 (%)	4.8	6.2	10.2

Source: Data compiled from various issues of *Automotive News*, 1989–90.

agement data that Ford outperformed GM in productivity, replacement time, factory utilization, and productivity increases in 1989. However, Ford still trails Toyota in all categories (Taylor 1990b).

Toyota Motors has established itself as the low-cost, high-quality, and best-value automobile producer among the top three. Toyota's cars cost $675 to $950 less to produce than those of Ford and GM (Treece and Howr 1989). In addition, Toyota leads Ford and GM in all high-speed management measures. Fewer worker hours are needed per car, it takes less time to replace a car, and, on average, Toyota workers are more productive than those at Ford and GM. That may be why Toyota has gone from 6 percent of the U.S. market in 1980 to 9 percent in 1990. In 1989, Toyota's market shares increased 3 percent in the United States, 3 percent in the European Community, and 4 percent in Japan, yielding a 10 percent increase worldwide, an increase in sales of more than a million cars (as mentioned above, a gain of a single percentage point amounts to 114,526 cars). While Ford and GM have lost market shares in the last ten years, Toyota has gained. According to Taylor (1990b), Toyota's innovative, adaptive, efficient, and rapid response systems account for the firm's competitive advantage in product cost, differentiation, scope, and timing.

Implications of Environmental Scanning and Value Chain Theory for High-Speed Management While environmental scanning and chain theory appear to be useful as analytic tools for exploring the types and sources of competitive advantage employed in the auto industry, two questions arise regarding the framework's generalizability:

1. Can the appropriate use of environmental scanning and value chain theory to analyze change in the environment and quickly adjust an organization's value chain to meet these changes separate successful from unsuccessful international competitors based on configuration and linking processes irrespective of industry?

2. Can environmental scanning and value chain theory demonstrate that firms that have a competitive advantage based on time also have improved performance ratings on all forms of competitive advantage?

Marquise Cvar (1986) attempted to answer the first question when he undertook a study of international corporations in 1984. For his research, Cvar selected eight successful and four unsuccessful firms. Of the successful firms, four were American and one each was Swiss, British, Italian, and French. Three of the four unsuccessful firms were American and one was Swiss. The studied firms competed in separate industries. Successful firms were distinguished from unsuccessful firms by their high investment in information and communication technology and by the effective use of information and communication to analyze and evaluate changes in the external organizational environment quickly and then to reorient its internal resources rapidly in responding to those changes.

Smith, Grimm, Chen, and Gannon (1989) attempted to answer the second question in their study of twenty-two top-level managers from high-technology electronics firms. They attributed major portions of the variance in organizational performance and increases in profits and sales to decreases in response time to environmental change. They found that an external orientation by a firm, a rapid response to competitor threat, and the radicalness of the change initiated in the organization were all positively related with communication systems improvements in an organization's R&D, manufacturing, and marketing.

Value chain theory does appear to be capable of *(a)* separating successful from unsuccessful international firms and *(b)* revealing how competitive advantage based on integration, coordination, and control proves overall organizational performance. While it is clear from our previous analysis that a successful global competitor carefully monitors changes in global economic forces and then quickly reorients the organization's value chain to meet those changes in ways that create value-added activities and thus competitive advantage, it is far from clear what philosophical rationale is for guiding the communication activities involved in these organizational adaptation processes. Fortunately, several well-developed studies have explored this problem in detail, with convergent results (Cvar 1986; Rockart and Short 1989; Smith et al. 1989; Venkatraman and Prescott 1990). They have all pointed to a philosophy that leads to the role that organizational teamwork plays as a communication response to the changes in the environment in order to create value-added activities and competitive advantage.

TEAMWORK AS A MAIN COMMUNICATION PROCESS IN HIGH-SPEED MANAGEMENT

In 1989, researchers at the Center for Information Systems Research at the MIT Sloan School of Management summarized these convergent studies when they stated that *an organization's ability to continuously improve its effectiveness in managing organizational interdependencies was the critical element in successfully responding to the competitive forces of the 1990s* (Rockart and Short 1989). *Effectiveness in managing organizational interdependencies refers to an organization's ability to achieve coalignment among its internal and external resources in a manner that is equal to or greater than existing world-class benchmarks for responding to environmental change.*

Coalignment is a unique form of organizational interdependence in which each of a firm's subunits or subsystems clearly articulates its needs, concerns, and potential contributions to the organization's functioning in such a manner that management can forge an appropriate value-added configuration and linkage between units. *An appropriate value-added configuration and linkage among units* is one that integrates, coordinates, and controls each unit's needs, concerns, and contributions so that the outcome is mutually satisfying to the units involved and optimizing in value-added activities to the organizational functioning as a whole.

Coalignment may occur at various levels, including, for example, technologies, equipment, funds, and human resources. Coalignment is operationalized through teamwork in which people use information and communication to manage interdependencies at all levels for achieving organizational goals. Or simply, teamwork is another way of saying coliagnment. Interorganizational teamwork is simply interorganizational coalignment. At the intraorganizational level, a self-managed team is that which executes self-managed coalignment; cross-functional teamwork is just cross-functional coalignment; and social technical teamwork is then social technical coalignment. Thus argued, *teamwork, in the context of high-speed management, is the effort to use information and communication to forge an appropriate value-added configuration and linkage between units so that firms are able to respond to the market environment with speed and create sustaining competitive advantage.* Or, to look at teamwork from the value chain perspective, teamwork is the use of information and communication to remove artificial barriers at both the functional and business process level of the value chain of an organization to achieve both organizational and interorganizational coalignment so that products may hit the market with speed and precision and gain high profits. While the use of information and communication to coalign design, engineering, purchasing, manufacturing, distribution, sales, and service constitutes intra-organizational teamwork, the communicative effort to achieve coalignment between an organization and its suppliers on the one hand and customers on the other is interorganizational teamwork. With speed-to-market as the main goal and all the challenges and stakes involved in mind, both intra- and interorganizational teamwork can be more or much more than mere talk.

CHAPTER 3

Speed-to-Market and International Benchmarking: Teamwork as a Goal-Oriented Action

> Faster, faster, faster! We're in a world that is obsessed with speed. "Time" has won the race to become our most valued resource—from the food we eat, whether it comes from a fast food restaurant or a microwave oven, to computers, airplanes and automobiles, pharmaceuticals, and even to written information. No longer is ordinary mail sufficient, now we have electronic mail. But why waste time typing. Just jot it down on a piece of paper and "FAX" it. Today, speed is everything.
>
> J. T. Vesey, "The New Competitors"

> Benchmarking is a process in which companies target key improvement areas within their firms, identify and study best practices by others in these areas, and implement new processes and system to enhance their own productivity and quality. Many leading companies are finding that in today's globally competitive market, you benchmark and improve—or you don't survive. Benchmarking, a continuous improvement process and partner of the total quality management (TQM), enables companies to look outside their own walls in the ongoing search for excellence.
>
> J. Kendrick, "Benchmarking Survey Builds Case for Looking to Others for TQM Models"

Nothing is worse than a high-speed management practice or process without a goal. Teamwork without goals will end up producing nothing but wasting resources. Teamwork in a high-speed business environment not only has goals, but has very high goals the achieving of which would help gain a firm sustainable competitive advantage. It is naive to believe that throwing five or six people into a group leads to teamwork, which then leads to organizational synergy and high performance. It is goals, or team members' firm commitment to the goals set, that drive the group to perform to their peak efficiency. In order to function effectively in a high-speed environment, teams must develop their goals at two levels. One is at the level of the general premises of high-speed management, and one is at the level of the firm's industry-market or business processes. The first level is a general level, which pertains to what is required of those who perceive themselves as players in the high-speed business environment. This is the general goal of speed-to-market with quality products or services. At the second level, a team has to develop its specific goals given the specific tasks it is assigned to perform. The setting of a team's specific goals depends very much on international benchmarking, which aims at locating the best practices in the world. It is therefore the task of this chapter to (1) identify some of the important functions that the general goal of speed-to-market plays in the teamwork process in a high-speed age and (2) explore the appropriate focus, strategies, techniques, and research regarding the effective use of benchmarking, investigate who the most effective benchmarkers are and how they proceed, and isolate the critical success factors that separate effective from ineffective benchmarking firms.

FUNCTIONS OF SPEED-TO-MARKET AS AN OVERALL GOAL IN TEAMWORK PROCESSES IN A HIGH-SPEED AGE

Speed-to-market is one of the central themes of this book and, indeed, one of the most important components of high-speed management as a new field of academic enquiry. We recall this theme over and over again throughout this book with a view to calling our readers' attention to its paramount importance. This is a theme that can never be overestimated from a high-speed management point of view. The mere fact that there is the word *speed* in the name of this new management and organizational communication philosophy, which is called high-speed management, points to the central place this theme occupies in this burgeoning field of study.

Speed-to-market as an overall goal for firms hard pressed by an increasingly competitive environment is a direct response to "rapidly changing technology, quick market saturation, unexpected competition" (Fraker 1984, p. 62). The following is already outdated information (any information could become outdated soon after it is printed in a high-speed age), but gives a simple explanation why speed-to-market has become an overall goal for competing firms: "General Electric used to take three weeks after an order to deliver a custom-made industrial circuit breaker box. Now it takes three days. AT & T used to need two years to design a new phone. Now it can do the job in one. Motorola used to turn out electronic pagers three weeks after the factory got the order. Now it takes two hours" (Dumaine 1989, p. 54). The urgency is well understood: if you don't speed up, you lose the competition to faster (and usually better) companies and die.

It seems that a shared perception of the importance of speed-to-market among organization members who work in a team setting affects teamwork process in a number of positive ways. So let's take a look at some of the functions that speed-to-market as an overall goal plays in the teamwork process in a high-speed age.

We can identify four major functions that the shared goal of speed-to-market plays in teamwork process in a high-speed age. First, it can help instill in team members a high sense of urgency of hitting the market with quality products or services. Second, it can lead to a high level of commitment and responsibility on the part of team members. Third, it can drive team members to accept high performance standards. And fourth, it can positively influence the composition of a team by recruiting the best people.

Sense of Urgency

According to Tom Peters (1987, p. 3), in a high-speed age, "no company is safe. IBM is declared dead in 1979, the best of the best in 1982, and dead again 1986. People Express is the model 'new look' firm, then flops twenty-four months later." He adds that "In 1987, and for the foreseeable future, there is no such thing as a 'solid,' or even substantial, lead over one's competitors. Too much is changing for anyone to be complacent." Where does IBM stand now at the time of the writing of these lines? It is now number 206, according to Fortune Magazine's 1993 list of America's Most Admired Corporations based on a study of 311 companies. IBM still fares better or much better than Wang Laboratories, which sits on the bottom of the Fortune list (Reese 1993). Wang Labs, which used to be one of the world's leaders in microprocessor technology, is now on the verge of bankruptcy. What is awaiting IBM in the years ahead? Nobody can tell for sure. What can be assured, however, is the fact that "the 'champ to chump' cycles are growing ever shorter—a 'commanding' advantage, such as Digital Equipment's current edge in networks that allow vast numbers of computers to interact with one another, is probably good for about eighteen months, at best" (Peters 1987, p. 3). This high-speed champ to chump (or chump to champ) cycle theory applies not just to Wang Labs or IBM; it applies to all companies. And that is the reality, a reality that is oftentimes hard to accept, but a reality that all companies must deal with for mere survival.

Keeping team members informed of what's been happening in the environment and what's been happening to the firm can help instill in them a sense of urgency, a sense of sharing, between the firm and individual members, the same life or death fate, a sense that, according to Benjamin Franklin, "if we don't hang together, we'll hang separately" (Barrett 1987, p. 24). It is really crucial to make it clear to all organization members that to achieve the goal of speed-to-market, you can't make the company do things just it does, only faster (Dumaine 1989, p. 55). *You have to revolutionize the way that things get done, and that's how you manage speed. Speed calls for change and excellence in performance, and speed, or rather, lack of speed, may kill a company.*

A High Level of Commitment

Teamwork is a condition; it comes and disappears. It takes a high level of commitment on the part of team members for the existing team to maintain its momentum until it is dissolved. Here *commitment* refers to the energy one is willing and ready to spend on the task he or she is assigned to perform. A high level of commitment is required of team members who are performing tasks in a high-speed business environment. Slacking off kills speed; this in turn may kill the company's competitive advantage. Therefore *a company's most effective call for team members' high level of commitment comes from their understanding of the volatile nature of the competitive environment, the company's position in the industry and the larger business space, and all the risks that are involved if the company fails to respond to the market contingencies with high speed.* It doesn't take a three-month training session to educate team members to understand why a high level of commitment is crucial for the company success; it just takes a brief reflection on the hard reality. But understanding is one thing, memorizing it and doing it is quite another.

An interesting example on hand is Domino's Pizza, which has become America's second-largest pizza chain (after Pizza Hut) by promising customers a $3 discount on any pie that takes longer than thirty minutes to arrive at their home. A delivery person, whose uniform includes track shoes, must run from the car to the house, taking stairs two at a time—elevators are forbidden because they take longer—carrying the pizza in his arms like a tailback headed for the goal line (Dumaine 1989, p. 9). This daily running exercise helps hammer the idea of speed into the delivery person's head. He understands and remembers the importance of running and therefore he keeps running, to deliver his pizza.

High Performance Standards

Benchmarking, which we will discuss in detail later in this chapter, is used to help teams to set up their specific performance standards. But speed-to-market as an overall goal should be employed to educate team members on the importance of setting high performance standards. High performance standards not only speed up the production of a particular product or service but improve or guarantee standards: "(1) customers—individual or industrial, high tech or low, science-trained or untrained—will pay a lot for better, and especially best, quality; moreover (2) firms that provide that quality will thrive; (3) workers in all parts of the organization will become energized by the opportunity to provide a top-quality product or service; and (4) no product has a safe quality lead, since new entrants are constantly redefining, for the customer, what's possible." Peters ridiculed corporate America by asking "So why does all this remain the best-kept secret in North America?" To raise the performance standards of all kinds of teams in organizations that are hard pressed by a high-speed environment, this "secret" must be made open to all who have a stake in the high-speed game.

Team Composition

The goal of speed-to-market puts a high pressure on team composition in terms of team members' skills and qualifications. To qualify as a candidate for joining a team that needs to meet the goal of speed-to-market, one must possess not only job skills, team and interaction skills, quality and problem solving skills but skills that would traditionally be required of a manager, skills of making tough decisions regarding reorientation of strategies for example. How a team is composed affects to a great extent the achieving of the overall goal of speed-to-market.

Having discussed the four functions that the general goal of speed-to-market can perform in teamwork process in a high-speed context, we are now in a position to lower our level of discussion to examine how specific goals should be developed for a team in an organization that is managed with high speed. We emphasize that we are not talking about the designing of specific goals for teams in a slow growth organization dealing with a stable or relatively stable environment. We are talking about teams working for an organization that has been gripped by a highly uncertain, fast-changing environment, an organization that desperately needs to keep up with the world class performance standards. In order for a team to come up with specific goals which are capable of matching with the industry's best practices, it must first of all perform benchmarking, as all successful companies have done. The remaining of the chapter is, therefore, devoted to a full discussion of how effective benchmarking can be practiced and its implications for the designing of specific goals for teams that are assigned to perform various tasks.

INTERNATIONAL BENCHMARKING

Port et al. (1992, p. 75) report that 90 percent of the firms leading their respective market segments in the Fortune International 500 survey attribute major portions of their competitive success to benchmarking. However, several recent studies conducted in Europe, Asia, and America report that most firms (70 percent of those reported) do not know how to effectively employ benchmarking practices to enhance organizational quality and productivity (Kendrick 1992, p. 1). In addition, many firms who attempt to utilize benchmarking practice invest lots of money and end up reducing quality and productivity (Fuchberg 1992b, p. B1). If benchmarking is such an important tool for leading edge firms, and if at the same time it is being so ineffectively employed by all except those leading edge firms, then it is imperative that we explore carefully its appropriate use. It will therefore be the purpose of this section to (1) explore the appropriate focus, strategies, techniques, and research regarding the effective use of benchmarking; (2) investigate who the most effective benchmarkers are and how they proceed; and (3) isolate the critical success factors that separate effective from ineffective benchmarking firms. Let us explore each of them in turn.

The Focus, Strategies, Techniques, and Research on Effective benchmarking

> Benchmarking benefits as a strategic planning method are that it identifies the key to success for each area studied, provides specific quantitative targets to shoot for, creates an awareness of state-of-the-art approaches, and helps companies cultivate a culture where change, adaptation, and continuous improvement are actively sought out.
>
> D. Altany, "Copycats"

In one sense, benchmarking's rapid ascent in importance is a surprise to some managers, because the process of benchmarking seems on the surface so straightforward and simple. A senior manager normally will start by deciding what part of an organization to benchmark. The manager then instructs the specialists in that area to map and begin collecting data on that process. Next, management locates a recognized world-class organization that excels in that same business process and offers to exchange information with it. After analyzing the data, a strategic plan is developed to incorporate the most effective approaches employed by the benchmarker firm. The simplicity of the process belies its true power and numerous pitfalls. In order to profit from the former and avoid the latter, we will explore benchmarking's (1) focus, strategies, and techniques and (2) the research available on its appropriate and inappropriate uses.

Benchmarking: Its Focus, Strategies, and Techniques Most theorists distinguish three types of benchmarking: (1) strategic, (2) process, and (3) customer (Jennings and Westfall 1992; Schmidt 1992).

Strategic benchmarking compares the success of different companies to one another in creating long-term value for shareholders with that of industrial peers. This is accomplished by measuring such factors as total shareholder return on assets, the ratio of a company's market value to book value, the positive spread in a firm's return on capital and its cost of capital and the value added productivity per employee, and so forth. Each of these measures provides some overall estimate of a firm's effectiveness in creating increased shareholder value given its general corporate strategy and allows a comparison among similar firms who employ differing strategies. For example, Ernst and Young (Port et al., Nov. 30, 1992) classified more than five hundred firms as novice, journeyman, and master based on their respective return on assets (ROA) and value added per employee (VAE).

Firms classified as novice have less than 2 percent ROA and less than $47,000 VAE. Firms classified as journeyman have 2 percent to 6.9 percent ROA and $47,000 to $73,999 VAE. Firms viewed as masters worthy of benchmarking had 7 percent or higher ROA and $74,000 or higher AVE (Port et al. 1992, p. 47). Others argue that the premier firms in the world, or the top international strategic benchmarks are best defined as those corporations that have earned more than their cost of capital every year for the past twenty years. Such a standard singles out only thirteen firms as valuable benchmarks. This select group includes American Home Products Corporation, General Electric, Philip Morris, and Rayathon from a wide range of industries (Schmidt 1992, p. 8). In each of these cases, a firm is attempting to locate world-class benchmarks by employing some overall measure of an organization's strategic effectiveness as measured against the best competitors in the world.

Process benchmarking on the other hand seeks to isolate one or more of a firm's primary business processes, that is, product development, billing and collection, integrated manufacturing, customer service, and so forth, and benchmark that process against a world-class competitor in regard to process and product cost, quality and speed-to-market, and so on. For example, Robert Camp, the manager of benchmarking competency at the Xerox Corporation, indicates that his firm operates in more than one hundred countries and performs benchmarking in each. Over the past ten years, the firms Xerox has process benchmarked against have grown. Camp reports:

> It includes the names of some of America's largest corporations, including American Express Co. (billing and collection); Ameri-

can Hospital Supply Co. (automated inventory control); Ford Motor Co. (manufacturing floor layout); General Electric Co. (robotics); L. L. Bean, Hershey Foods Corp. , and Mary Kay Cosmetics, Inc. (warehousing and distribution); Westinghouse Electric Corp. (National Quality Award application process, warehouse controls, and bar coding); and Florida Power and Light Co. (quality process). (Camp 1992, p. 3)

In addition, Xerox's Fuji, Japan, facility won the 1990 Deming Award from the Japanese government for manufacturing quality. It therefore frequently employs internal benchmarking whereby its manufacturing affiliates in Europe, the United States, and Africa benchmark their manufacturing practices against Xerox's affiliate in Japan. Both Xerox's top management and Robert Camp attribute Xerox's increased market shares and return to dominance in the photocopying field to the success of its international benchmarking of business process (Camp 1989).

Customer benchmarking involves surveying one's customers regarding what qualities one's own firm and one's competitors' product attributes they consider the most important in influencing their purchase of a product. Then, given this attribute list, a firm benchmarks those attributes and competing firms' product attributes in order to add them to their own product. Customer benchmarking is a four-step process:

1. identify the attributes that influence customer value perceptions
2. assess corporate performance
3. analyze competitors' performance and standing
4. close gaps between current performance and customer expectation

For example, the Chrysler Corporation recently designed its new LH auto series by benchmarking the best attributes of other automobiles in the world. Chrysler took more than two hundred dream attributes by customers of their ideal car and benchmarked them. They studied the Acura Legend and Nissan Maxima for suspension systems, the BMW for ventilation and heating, and so forth, and then they designed a car with the best combination of these features available for its price range (Scarr 1992, p. A1). The emergent design is aimed at recapturing Chrysler's lost market shares in the mid-price range auto market. Customer benchmarking has been listed by such firms as Xerox, Motorola, Chrysler, and GM as a key strategy for regaining lost market shares in their respective competitive markets.

Strategic, process, and *customer* benchmarking against world-class competitors has become a major organizational tool for restoring firms to a position of excellence and increased stockholder value, business process excellence, and market shares in the global marketplace.

The actual processes involved in implementing a best practices program are varied. Xerox, one of the earlier firms to systematically employ benchmarking employs a ten-step, four stages process (see fig. 3.1)

Underlying this ten-step, four-stage process are several well developed fundamental activities.

1. Know your own operation and carefully assess its strengths and weaknesses.
2. Locate world-class leaders and competitors to benchmark against.
3. Measure carefully productivity, quality, and speed-to-market.
4. Analyze carefully how and why the benchmark is different from yours.
5. Incorporate and improve on the best practices to gain superiority.
6. Continuously update benchmarking of your organization's central competitive processes.
7. Remember, in the final analysis, the customer is the best judge of how good you are.

When unsuccessful, this benchmarking process normally fails at *(a)* the measurement phase, *(b)* the analysis of difference phase, and *(c)* in the cost of the benchmarking process given its benefits to the firm. For example, the International Benchmarking Clearinghouse surveyed more than eighty companies and found that the average time and cost per benchmarking team per project was 878 hours per team member; that is, more than 14 1/2 weeks per person, with the full cost per project averaging $67,857. Given

FIGURE 3.1
The Benchmarking Process

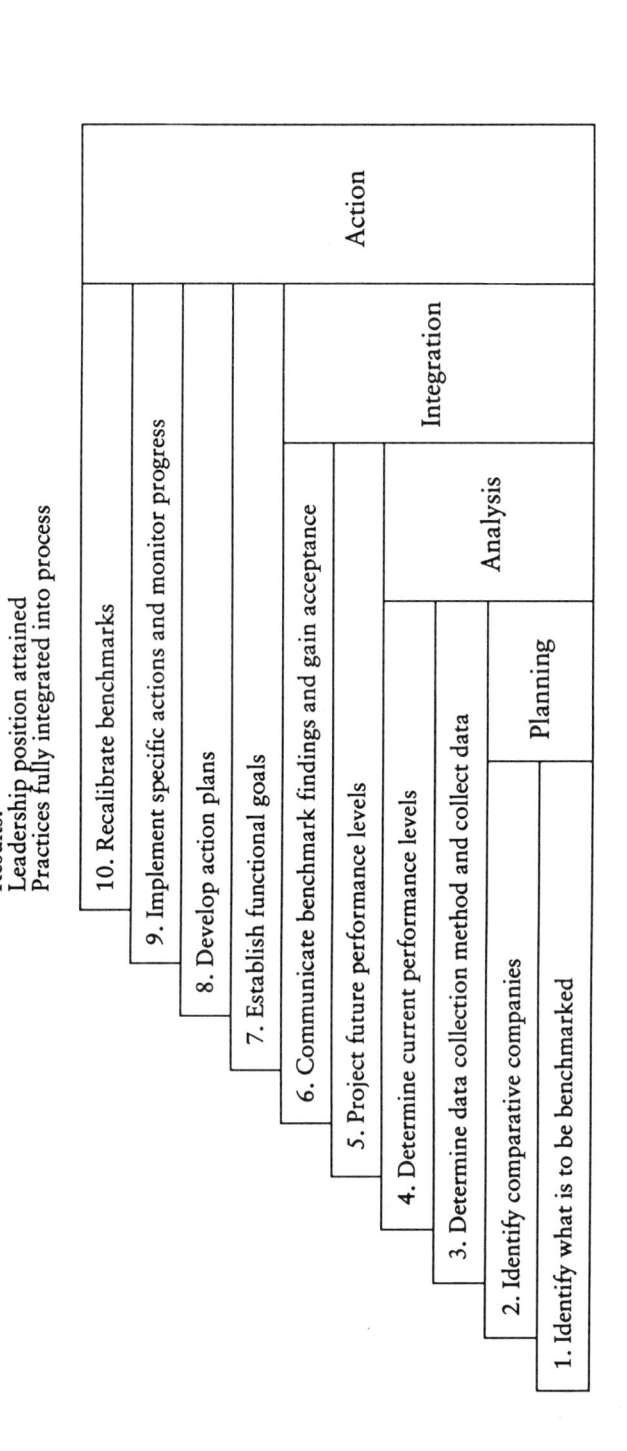

Results:
Leadership position attained
Practices fully integrated into process

10. Recalibrate benchmarks
9. Implement specific actions and monitor progress
8. Develop action plans
7. Establish functional goals
6. Communicate benchmark findings and gain acceptance
5. Project future performance levels
4. Determine current performance levels
3. Determine data collection method and collect data
2. Identify comparative companies
1. Identify what is to be benchmarked

Action
Integration
Analysis
Planning

Source: Adapted from Camp 1992, p. 4.

such a hefty up-front investment, a firm must be careful to recover it's costs from it's efforts (Wiesamdanger 1992, p. 63).

Research Finding on the Appropriate Use of Benchmarking In spite of the importance of benchmarking to organizational survival, recent studies reveal that most organizations do not effectively employ organizational benchmarking to enhance their quality and productivity. The American Productivity and Quality Centers International Benchmarking Clearinghouse (IBC) surveyed seventy-six member organizations in 1992. The major findings included:

- Most firms, 90 percent, consider benchmarking as a necessary tool for survival; however, most of the firms feel they don't know how to do it well.
- Eighty-three percent consider themselves beginner or novice users, with nearly half employing benchmarking less than two years.
- Only 51 percent have conducted two to five process benchmarking studies. However, industry leading corporations had conducted twenty or more such studies, many on a regular basis.
- Most important skills for benchmarking firms to master are process analysis, communication, and team functioning.
- Ninety-three percent report top management support, 80 percent use model steps, and 94 percent use team approach. (Kendrick 1992, p. 1)

Ernst and Young reported the results of a five-year study of quality control in more than five hundred firms. They concluded that only top performing firms have the internal skills, financial resources, and know-how to successfully benchmark the world's best firms. For an overview of their findings, please refer back to table 1.2 on page 00.

In short, the Ernst and Young study concludes that only master firms, firms with an ROA of 7 percent and higher and a VAE of $74,000 and up have the skills, knowledge, and resources to measure, analyze, and implement correctly superior business practices, and only they can afford the $70,000 average cost for such benchmarking processes.

Who Are the Most Effective Benchmarkers, and How Do They Proceed?

> A lot of companies are internally focused and just have not thought about going outside the company to get information. . . . Some of these managers are locked into the mentality of improving only on last year's performance by 10 percent, and don't realize that another company might be 100 percent or even 1000 percent more efficient than they are in certain functions. By not indemnifying those areas and learning more efficient techniques, they remain behind. Company goals should always be geared towards being the best in the world, rather than just slightly better than last year.
>
> Jim Sierk, Vice President of Quality at Xerox Corporation

If international benchmarking of world-class competitors is at once essential to competitive success and very difficult to implement successfully except for world-class competitors, how is a firm to proceed? Two issues arise that warrant our attention: (1) how do we learn how to be a world-class benchmarker? and (2) what firms and in what areas can and do we need to benchmark? Let us explore each of these issues in turn.

How Do We Learn How to Be a World-Class Benchmarker? Only recently have organizational practices begun to reveal a method for non-leading edge firms to develop world-class benchmarking capabilities. These practices involve (1) the use of internal benchmarking, (2) involvement in a benchmarking clearinghouse, and (3) competition for The Baldridge Award as progressive stages in developing world-class benchmarking skills.

Internal Benchmarking Experience teaches us that conducting internal benchmarking studies of several of one's own business processes can provide an inexpensive laboratory for the initial development of benchmarking skills. A firm begins by selecting a benchmarking team from the areas to be benchmarked and seeks outside consultants to train them in beginning benchmarking skills. The team then attempts to figure out how to measure, analyze, evaluate, and implement a best practices program between two or more functionally similar units of one's own firm. In addition, this is an excellent first step toward understanding one's own strategic, process, and customer benchmarking. Such studies can be done in one-fifth of the time and at one-fourth of the cost of external benchmarking.

Involvement in a Benchmarking Clearinghouse After making several attempts at internal benchmarking, a firm should send its benchmarking teams to participate in the training and practice sessions of a benchmarking clearinghouse. Such clearinghouses provide intermediate training in benchmarking skills and an opportunity to study other non-leading-edge firms. While the cost of such studies is slightly higher than internal benchmarking, it is less than competitive leading edge benchmarking. Several firms exist internationally to provide such services.

Competing for the Baldridge Award In the United States each year several quality awards are presented to leading edge firms. The national Baldridge Award is one such contest. Table 3.1 lists the scoring process for winning the Baldridge Award presented to leading edge firms. The award competition is a five-to-ten-year climb into the arena of world-class benchmarkers. Past award winners have gone on to lead their respective market segments, develop world-class business processes, and become world leaders in strategic benchmarking.

TABLE 3.1
Scoring the 1991 Baldridge Award
(1,000 total points)

1.0 Leadership (100 points)
- 1.1 Senior executive leadership (40)
- 1.2 Quality values (15)
- 1.3 Management for quality (25)
- 1.4 Public responsibility (20)

2.0 Information and Analysis (70 points)
- 2.1 Scope and management of quality data and information (20)
- 2.2 Competitive comparisons and benchmarks (30)
- 2.3 Analysis of quality data and information (20)

3.0 Strategic Quality Planning (60 points)
- 3.1 Strategic quality planning process (35)
- 3.2 Quality goals and plans (25)

4.0 Human Resources Utilization (150 points)
- 4.1 Human resource management (20)
- 4.2 Employee involvement (40)

TABLE 3.1 (continued)

4.3 Quality education and training (40)
4.4 Employee recognition and performance measurement (25)
4.5 Employee well-being and morale (25)

5.0 Quality Assurance of Products and Services (140 points)
  5.1 Design and introduction of quality products and service (35)
  5.2 Process quality control (20)
  5.3 Continuous improvement of processes (20)
  5.4 Quality assessment (15)
  5.5 Documentation (10)
  5.6 Business process and support service quality (20)
  5.7 Supplier quality (20)

6.0 Quality Results (180 points)
  6.1 Product and service quality results (90)
  6.2 Business process, operational, and support service quality results (50)
  6.3 Supplier quality results (40)

7.0 Customer Satisfaction (300 points)
  7.1 Determining customer requirements and expectations (30)
  7.2 Customer relationship management (50)
  7.3 Customer service standards (20)
  7.4 Commitment to customers (15)
  7.5 Complaint resolution for quality improvement (25)
  7.6 Determining cusstomer satisfaction (20)
  7.7 Customer satisfaction results (70)
  7.8 Customer satisfaction comparison (70)

What Firms and In What Areas Do We Benchmark? Benchmarking is a tool for assessing the best practices of others and using the resulting stretch objectives as design criteria for upgrading one's own performance. Strategic benchmarking attempts to extend this process throughout an organization in order to achieve sustainable competitive advantage. Tables 3.2 and 3.3 list some world-class benchmarking candidates by business processes.

Most of these world-class performers benchmark each other and regularly share benchmarking data. Some of these data are made available to clearinghouses and some are not. However,

TABLE 3.2
World-Class Benchmarking Candidates I

Automated inventory control	Westinghouse Apple Computer Federal Express
Billing and collection	American Express MCI
Customer service	Xerox Nordstrom Inc. L. L. Bean
Environmental management	3M Ben & Jerry's Dow Chemical
Health-care management	Coors Southern California Edison Allied Signal
Manufacturing operations management	Hewlett-Packard Corning Inc. Phillip Morris
Marketing	Helene Curtis The Limited Microsoft
Product development	Motorola Digital Equipment Sony 3M
Purchasing	Honda Motor Xerox NCR
Quality process	Westinghouse Florida Power & Light Xerox
Robotics	General Electric
Sales management	IBM Procter & Gamble Merck

TABLE 3.2 (continued)

Technology transfer	Square D 3M Dow Chemical
Training	Ford General Electric Polaroid
Warehousing and distribution	L. L. Bean Hershey Foods Mary Kay Cosmetics

Source: Altany 1990, p. 12.

TABLE 3.3
World-Class Benchmarking Candidates II

Benchmarking	Xerox Motorola Ford Florida Power & Light IBM/Rochester DEC
Billing and collection	American Express MCI
Customer focus	Xerox GE (plastics) Wallace Co. Westinghouse (furniture systems)
Design for manufacturing assembly	Motorola DEC NCR
Employee suggestions	Millikin Dow Chemical Toyota
Empowerment	Millikin Honda of America
Flexible manufacturing	Allen-Bradly/Milwaukee Baldor Electric

TABLE 3.3 (continued)
World-Class Benchmarking Candidates II

Industrial design	Black & Decker (household products) Braun Herman Miller
Leadership	GE: Jack Welch Hanover Insurance: Bill O'Brien Manco Inc.: Jack Kahl
Marketing	Procter & Gamble
Quality process	Wallace Co. Florida Power & Light Toyota IBM/Rochester
Quick changeover	United Electric Controls Dana Corp./Minneapolis Johnson Controls/Milwaukee
R&D	AT&T Hewlett-Packard Shell Oil
Self-directed work team	Corning/SCC Plant Physio Control Toledo Scale
Supplier management	Levi Strauss Motorola Xerox Ford 3M Bose Corp.
Total productive maintenance	Tennessee Eastman
Training	Wallace Co. Square D
Waste minimization	3M Dow Chemical

Source: Altany 1991, p. 15.

access to those world-class firms is restricted, unless you have something they want and are willing to share. Let us explore one attempt at such a sharing process between a large world-class Japanese firm and a small American firm.

The Danville, Illinois, Bumper Works In 1978, Shahid Khan, a naturalized U.S. citizen from Pakistan, borrowed $50,999 from the Small Business Loan Corporation and took $16,000 of his own savings to establish the one-hundred-employee Bumper Works in Danville, Illinois. This company designed and manufactured truck bumpers. Between 1980 and 1985, Khan approached the Toyota Motor Corporation on several occasions, attempting to become a supplier of bumpers for their trucks but without much success.

In 1987, the Toyota Motor Company called together a group of one hundred potential suppliers and released their design, quality, quantity, and price range specifications for the truck bumpers. The officials at Toyota also indicated that they expected increased quality and a reduction in price each year from the supplier. By 1988, only Khan's Bumper Works company could produce a product that met Toyota's exacting requirements.

In 1989, Toyota Motor Company sent a manufacturing team to Danville, Illinois, to negotiate the contract and coalignment agreement between the two firms. The negotiations failed because the Bumper Works could not produce twenty different-sized bumpers and ship them in a single day. If Bumper Works could not do this, Toyota's truck production would slow down, since a single batch production line was used for all Toyota trucks. The truck price would increase dramatically (White 1991, pp. A1, A7).

Khan called a "town meeting" of workers from his own and Toyota Motor's Japanese factories to explore how this problem might be solved within Toyota's design, quality, quantity, and price requirements. It was decided that Bumper Works would have to switch the factory from a mass production to a batch production line and that a massive stamping machine that took ninety minutes to change each cutting die would have to be modified so as to make such changes in 20 minutes (p. A7).

Next, the workers at both Bumper Works and Toyota set up cross-functional teams to make a process map of current production procedures. They studied, simplified, and restructured the process so as to allow for batch production. The large stamping machine was studied for modifications that would speed up die changes. All this was done with considerable help from Toyota, which had solved these same problems, but in different way, back in Japan (p. A7).

Then, the Bumper Works's remodeled assembly line was ready to begin production. For six months employees with stop watches and cost sheets observed the restructured process and benchmarked its operations against the world-class standards of Toyota Plant in Japan—but still could not meet Toyota's quality, quantity, and speed of delivery specifications. They videotaped the process, studied it, and sent it to Japan for review. In July 1990 Toyota sent a team over to help retrain the workers. They returned again in December 1990 to fine tune the process, meeting Toyota Motor's contract requirements.

The new production line increased productivity more than 60 percent above the previous year, decreased defects 80 percent, cut delivery time by 850 percent, and reduced waste materials cost by 50 percent. A manual and videotape of the manufacturing process, the first of their kind at Bumper Works, were prepared for training, and continuous improvement teams were formed in order to meet contract requirements for Toyota of increased quality and decreased costs.

The representatives of each unit involved in the value chain linking Bumper Works and Toyota had communicated their interests, concerns, and contributions to the coalignment process. Each firm's management, therefore, was able to forge a linking process that was satisfactory and optimizing to the value-added activities of each organization, creating a sustainable competitive advantage. Khan, the owner of Bumper Works, has profited from this experience and is building a new plant that will employ two hundred workers in Indiana and will supply truck bumpers for a new Isuzu Motors plant located there (p. A7).

Critical Success Factors for International Benchmarking

> The Japanese word *dantotsy* means striving to be the best of the best. It captures the essence of benchmarking, which is a positive, proactive process designed to change operations in a structured fashion to achieve superior performance. The purpose of benchmarking is to increase the probability of success of an attempt to gain a competitive advantage.
>
> R. Camp, "Learning from the Best Leads to Superior Performance"

World-class benchmarking is an essential tool for cutting edge firms, a tool that is difficult to acquire the appropriate skills to employ. However, once the skills have been developed and employed, they are what separate world-class performers from also-rans. The acquisition and development of such skills normally follow a three-stage acquisition process:

1. internal benchmarking
2. clearinghouse participation
3. competitive participation in the Baldridge Award

This three-stage process involves practice in three types of benchmarking with world-class competitors:

1. strategic benchmarking
2. process benchmarking
3. customer benchmarking

These three types of benchmarking all employ a four-stage process:

1. planning
2. analysis
3. integration
4. action

In all of these stages, successful benchmarking depends on the appropriate measurement, analysis, and implementation of other firms' best practices.

CHAPTER 4

Defining Qualities and Dominant Patterns of Teamwork

As has been indicated in chapter 2, high-speed management as a new theory of organizational communication is a set of principles, strategies, and tools for coming up with a steady flow of new products, making sure they are what the customer wants, designing and manufacturing them with speed and precision, getting them to the market quickly, and servicing them easily in order to make large profits and satisfy consumer needs. This new theory has at its core a new conceptualization of the role information and communication play in organizational functioning (Cushman and King 1993; Pepper 1989). Cushman and King (1993) identify four communication processes, which they argue are crucial for establishing and maintaining a firm's sustainable competitive advantage. Two of them are, either in a direct or extended sense, no more than teamwork processes: (1) a negotiated linking process, and (2) a cross-functional teamwork process. While they are by no means the only teamwork processes applied in organizational functioning, they are typical of two broad categories of organizational coalignment in a high-speed management age, that is, interorganizational teamwork and intraorganizational teamwork.

This chapter discusses defining qualities and dominant patterns of organizational teamwork in the context of high-speed management. Such a discussion is grounded in the core philoso-

---

Portions of this chapter were presented at the corporate Communication Conference held at Fairleigh Dickinson University in May 1992 and published in M. Cross and W. Cummins, eds., *The Proceedings of the Fifth Conference on Corporate Communication*, Fairleigh Dickinson University, Madison, N.J., 1992; reprinted in S. King and D. P. Cushman, eds., *High-Speed Management and Organizational Communication in the 1990s: A Reader* (Albany: SUNY Press, 1994).

phy implied in effective organizational functioning as the conceptual basis for the role that teamwork plays in high-speed management (for a review of this core philosophy, refer back to chapter 2). This discussion is also built on the basis of chapter 3, which discusses teamwork as that which facilitates and, in turn, is driven by speed-to-market and international benchmarking. Therefore, *teamwork is conceptualized not only as a usable management tool in a normal sense but as a goal-driven value-added process critical for organizational survival and the maintenance of sustainable competitive advantage.* The main task of this chapter is to identify teamwork qualities and patterns that have become most successfully tested in businesses and organizations following high-speed management principles and strategies. *These are the qualities of consistency, intensity, permanent dissatisfaction, and speedy and effective communication. As far as the dominant teamwork patterns are concerned, there are cross-functional teamwork, self-managed teamwork, executive-level teamwork, and social-technical teamwork.* Following our discussion of the four teamwork qualities and four dominant teamwork patterns in the context of high-speed management will be two case studies on two of the world's most successful organizations applying teamwork, the Toyota Motor Company in Japan and General Electric (GE) in the United States. Then relying upon our comparison of the two success stories, the detailed discussions of the high-speed management philosophy in chapter 2 and speed-to-market in chapter 3, we will present a model of teamwork intended to be used in the context of high-speed management. This model, which is subject to test, hopefully, will help businesses and organizations to improve their teamwork design and practices so that they can compete on a new level in today's high-speed environment.

As we have pointed out in chapter 3, teamwork can never really be effective without some clearly identified and articulately defined goals in the minds of team players. And one such goal for high-speed management teamwork in business organizations is speed-to-market. Crucial to achieving speed-to-market is, among other critical factors, the effective use of information and communication to remove all the artificial barriers that lie along the value chain of an organization. The value chain, which involves all the essential functional units and discrete activities, may be arranged into functional unit activities and business processes (Cushman and King 1993a). At the functional unit level, the value chain starts from suppliers and runs through design, engineering, purchasing, manufacturing, distribution, sales, and service, and ends at customers. Suppliers and customers at the two ends are found outside an organization's boundary, while all other functional activities are performed within its structure. This suggests that the removal of barriers, through the sharing of information and a supportive communication climate, should occur at both the organizational and interorganizational levels. The business process of the value chain includes three stages: product development, product delivery, and customer service and management. Each stage has some activities unique to itself and some activities that overlap with other business processes. This demands a smooth linkage and transition among the three business processes, implying that all obstacles need to be removed as soon as they emerge.

Based on our conceptualization of teamwork as coalignment among functional units and activities at the beginning of this chapter, it seems natural to claim that the very removal of artificial barriers at both the functional unit level and business process level of the value chain constitutes teamwork. This is to say that teamwork is the use of information and communication to remove artificial barriers that lie along the value chain of an organization to achieve both organizational and interorganizational coalignment so that products may hit the market with speed and precision and gain high profits. *The use of information and communication to coalign design, engineering, purchasing, manufacturing, distribution, sales, and service constitutes intraorganizational teamwork, while the communicative effort to achieve coalignment between an organization and its suppliers on the one hand and its customers on the other is interorganizational teamwork.* With speed-to-market as the main goal and all the challenges and stakes involved in mind, both intra- and interorganizational teamwork can be more or much more than mere talk. We are now in a position to take a closer look at defining qualities and dominant patterns of teamwork in high-speed management.

DEFINING QUALITIES OF TEAMWORK

Kinlaw argues that "teamwork is a condition that may come and go. It may exit only for the time that it takes a group to perform a particular task; after the task is performed, the need for teamwork no longer exists. Group members can have teamwork one moment, then be disjunctive and at odds with each other the next. People can rally around some purpose and cooperate to achieve it, then break up and become very competitive and proprietary" (Kinlaw 1991, pp. 1–2). He describes teamwork as consisting of both qualitative characteristics and functional characteristics. *The qualitative characteristics of teamwork include quality communication climate and positive work relationships, while the functional characteristics pertain to a team or an organization's functional goals that team members need to work together to achieve, such as the producing of a product or service that cannot be produced by a single person or department.* Based upon these teamwork characteristics, Kinlaw distinguishes work groups from work teams and work teams from superior work teams (pp. 6–7). Let's elaborate.

Work Groups

A work group is a set of two or more jobholders who make up some identifiable organizational unit that is considered to be a permanent part of an organization. Work groups are the basic building blocks of organizational performance. *The tasks of individual members in groups may be performed through processes that are additive, integrative, or interactive.* Various combinations of these three processes can all be effective depending on conditions. In *additive processes*, workers in the same group all use the same equipment or machine to produce the same product. The group's output is not integrated into a larger whole. Individual outputs are added together, and the sum total becomes the group's output. *Integrative processes* are typically used by production-line groups, where what a member does at an earlier stage is not simply added but integrated into work that is done at later stages. All members of the group and all parts of the work, which often follows a one-way, linear path, are interdependent. In *interactive processes*, the job gets done neither through a simple addition of individual outputs nor through a one-way, linear integration of work parts but through a two-way or multidirection flow of information and action among individual members of the group. Design groups, budget groups, R&D groups, and the like are typically interactive. The additive processes, integrative processes, and interactive processes are compared in figure 4.1.

FIGURE 4.1
Work Group Task Flows

Additive
Task^1 + Task^2 + Task^3 + ... + Task^n = Summary Result
(Task 1 ... N)

Integrative
Task^1 + Task^2 + Task^3 + ... + Task^n = Integrative Result
(Task 1 ... N)

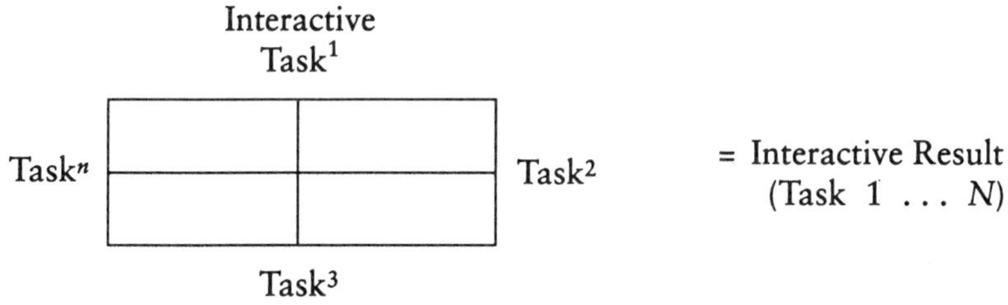

Interactive
Task^1

Task^n ⎯⎯ Task^2 = Interactive Result
(Task 1 ... N)

Task^3

Source: Kinlaw 1991, p. 9.

According to Kinlaw (1991), a work group that uses additive processes alone to produce a product or service may function without teamwork. Integrative and interactive processes, which obviously would require coalignment between team members, force at least minimal levels of teamwork. This is to say that groups whose tasks are integrative and/or interactive by nature must function as teams.

Work Teams and Superior Work Teams

Kinlaw argues that teams differ from groups at two levels. *At the qualitative level, teams tend to have a quality communication climate in which sharing information is easier, issues are aired more openly, and conflicts are resolved quickly and with positive results. At the functional level, members of a work team not only cooperate in all aspects of their task performance; they also share functions and responsibilities that traditionally belong to management.*

According to Kinlaw, *superior work teams, in addition to having the same functional and qualitative characteristics as work teams, are defined by three qualities: consistency, intensity, and restless dissatisfaction.* Consistency means that superior work teams are consistent in their pursuit of excellence, and *"always* make maximum use of their people; *always* achieve superior outputs against all odds; and *always* are improving every aspect of their business" (Kinlaw 1991, p. 16). In other words, they consistently work in such a way as to maintain sustaining competitive edge. *Intensity* refers to the high level of energy and commitment in performing team tasks. *Restless dissatisfaction* reflects the belief on the part of team members that nothing is so good that cannot be improved.

The three qualities of consistency, intensity, and restless dissatisfaction combine to suggest that superior work teams are teams that perform high-speed management teamwork. Integrating Cushman and King's framework of high-speed management and Kinlaw's conceptualization of work groups versus work teams versus superior work teams, *we view high-speed management teamwork as having the characteristics of consistency, intensity, restless (we will change the word to* permanent *later in the chapter) dissatisfaction, and—we may now add one more—speedy and effective communication, as shown in the efforts of individual members of superior work teams which perform mainly integrative and interactive tasks.* Such tasks are performed along the whole value chain of an organization at both the functional unit level and business process level.

DOMINANT TEAMWORK PATTERNS

High-speed management teamwork may appear in different forms, at different hierarchical levels, and across different function units along the value chain. We now use the four qualities of consistency, intensity, permanent dissatisfaction, and speedy and effective communication as the cross-cutting themes to look at the four teamwork patterns: cross-functional teamwork, self-managed teamwork, executive-level teamwork, and social technical teamwork.

Cross-functional Teamwork

Increases in information and communication technological breakthroughs and in world trade in the past decade have created a volatile business climate characterized by rapidly changing technology, quick market saturation, and unexpected competition, making succeeding in business very difficult (Cushman and King 1993a). Technological changes with increased competition have required companies to become more market driven, to attempt to gain competitive advantage by reaching the marketplace first with a superior product. As a result, organizations are turning to project management and relying to a greater degree on project teams and cross-functional teamwork for the development and implementation of new products and programs (Pinto and Pinto 1990).

Cross-functional teamwork in high-speed management may be defined as a team process where members from different functional units work together with a team spirit of consistency, intensity, permanent dissatisfaction, and speedy and effective communication to complete some project within a certain time limit, or to achieve organizational goals without a specific time constraint. Earlier research on cross-functional teamwork has tended to focus on one function's specific relationship with other functional areas, examining the dynamics of these relationships as well as that function's specific responsibilities regarding new product implementation. These relationships have included, for example, marketing and R&D, marketing and production, marketing and engineering, and marketing and finance (Pinto and Pinto 1990; Gupta and Wileman 1988; Clare and Sanford 1984; Anderson 1981). Researchers have also inquired into various behavioral issues such as problems of personality differences among members of functional units who worked on the same project (Lucas and Bush 1988).

What seems to be largely neglected in researchers' conceptualization of cross-functional teamwork has been the emphasis on non-project oriented, general organizational goals driven interdependencies among all the functional units along the value chain of an organization. This simply means that *the spirit of cross-functional teamwork should exist in the whole organization and involve all functional units on a routine, day-to-day basis.* Here is introduced the principle of *consistency*, which, as we pointed out earlier, emphasizes "always, always, and always." It goes without saying that project-based cross-functional teamwork is of paramount importance to a high-speed management organization that needs superior products with which to hit the marketplace with speed. It is also worth emphasizing, however, that an organization that faces an uncertain and volatile business environment should be ready to act with big moves any time if need be. But this would be very difficult or simply impossible if the level of coalignment among various functional units along the value chain were not kept consistently high. The principle of consistency also applies to project-based cross-functional teamwork, where a project team would need to function as a superior work team at both qualitative and functional levels from the time the team is formed to the time it is dissolved in a consistent way.

The quality of *intensity*, as it is also required of cross-functional teamwork in high-speed management organizations, suggests that team members need to maintain a high level of energy and commitment. A high-level commitment on the part of members of different functional units is probably easier said than made. Commitment is more likely to come from stakeholders' true and profound understanding of the significance and importance of project-based as well as routine cross-functional teamwork for the organization. Once commitment is made, energy comes naturally.

Permanent dissatisfaction is even a higher demand of individual workers who might say "why bother?" Members of work groups then need to be educated into becoming team players by using such arguments as "if we don't hang together, we'll hang separately" (Barrett 1987, p. 24). Too easy a satisfaction with a product or service in a high-speed business environment could send you and all other organization members to dance on the rope.

Speedy and effective communication is not only a tool with which to help promote team qualities of consistency, intensity, and permanent dissatisfaction, but a necessary element of teamwork at both the qualitative and functional levels. At the qualitative level, there is the need for establishing and maintaining a quality communication climate in which different opinions are voiced in a supportive, unreserved, and timely way. At the functional level, team roles and goals need to be clarified and updated, again using speedy and effective communication to render high-speed management cross-functional teamwork a goal-driven, value-added process, not just managerial lip-service.

Self-managed Teamwork

Self-managed teamwork has been a new and effective response to the high-speed management environment in which technological breakthroughs present repeated challenges to firms, markets become saturated quickly, and competition comes from all directions, an environment that demands organizational innovation, adaptation, flexibility, efficiency, and rapid response (Cushman and King 1993a). The use of self-managed teams to respond to such an environment not only has gained momentum but appears to be at a record high. Self-managed teamwork appears in such team forms as quality control circles, task forces, communication teams, new venture teams, and business brand teams (Barry 1991).

Wellins and George (1991) report that a recent nationwide study conducted jointly by Development Dimensions International (DDI), the Association for Quality and Participation (AQP), and *Industry Week* reveals that 26 percent of the 862 executives surveyed are using self-managed teamwork in at least some parts of their organizations and that more than half of their workforces will be organized into self-managed teams within five years. It has been reported that self-managed teams, if well managed, tend to produce good outcomes in both terms of productivity and member satisfaction (e.g., Hackman and Oldham 1980; Hackman et al. 1975)

Organizations that heavily depend on the use of self-managed teamwork differ from traditional organizations in a number of ways, including that (1) the former are usually leaner, with fewer layers of managers and supervisors; (2) the leader is more a coach than a planner and controller; (3) the reward systems tend to be skill- or team-based, rather than seniority-based; (4) information, such as productivity data, quality data, sales figures, and profit margins, is shared readily with all employees, not just the top few; (5) and employees are expected to learn all the jobs and tasks required of the team, not just a single job or task (Wellins and George 1991). All these differences suggest that organizations dependent upon self-managed teamwork are those that follow high-speed management principles in order to respond more speedily and efficiently to a volatile business environment.

As is implied in the name, *self-managed teamwork is leaderless in the traditional sense of the word* leader. *This does not mean, however, that leadership is not exercised in self-managed work teams. In many ways, the opposite holds true.* Barry (1991) argues that *self-managed teams require even more leadership than conventional organizational units.* They need not only task-based leadership on such critical issues as project definition, scheduling, and resource-gathering, but also leadership around group development processes, including developing group cohesiveness and establishing effective communication patterns. Barry also points out that without the presence of formal authority, power struggles and conflict around both task and group process issues develop more often, adding to the overall leadership burden that must be handled by all members of the group. To explain, predict, or control leadership complexities in self-managed teams, Barry (1991) proposes a new leadership theory called "Distributed Leadership Model" (DLM) which he believes is uniquely suited to self-managed teamwork. DLM sees leadership as "a collection of roles and behaviors that can be split apart, shared, rotated, and used sequentially or concomitantly," and this means that "at any one time multiple leaders can exist in a team, with each leader assuming a complementary leadership role" (p. 34). Such leadership roles and behaviors as required of self-managed work teams, according to Barry, fall into four broad clusters. The first is *envisioning leadership*, a process involving "facilitating idea generation and innovation, defining and championing overall goals, finding conceptual links between systems, and fostering frame-breaking thinking" (p. 36). The second is *organizing leadership*, which "brings order to the many disparate elements that exist within the group's tasks" and focuses on "details, deadlines, time, efficiency, and structure" (p. 36). *Spanning leadership* represents the third cluster. This deals with how to bridge and link the team with outside groups and individuals, involving such behaviors as "networking, presentation management, developing and maintaining a strong team image with outsiders, intelligence gathering, locating and securing critical resources, bargaining, finding and forecasting areas of outside resistance, being sensitive to power distributions, and being politically astute" (p. 37). The fourth cluster is *social leadership*. While the first three clusters of leadership pertain to task performance, social leadership is exercised in group development processes, which include "surfacing different members' needs and concerns, assuring that everyone gets his or her views heard, interpreting and paraphrasing other views, being sensitive to the team's energy levels and emotional state, injecting humor and fun into the team's work, and being able to mediate conflicts" (p. 37).

The fact that these extremely challenging leadership roles must be assumed by team members themselves suggests that the staffing and training of self-managed teams could be critical to ensure their success. This is simply because not all workers are capable of assuming leadership roles, and not all workers perform well in a team environment (Flynn, McCombs, and Elloy 1990). *To tie our discussion to the context of high-speed management, we suggest that the four qualities of high-speed management teamwork, that is, consistency, intensity, permanent dissatisfaction, and speedy and effective communication, be used as basic criteria with which to select and train members of self-managed teams.* Consistency means "always." If one is entrusted, for example, with assuming envisioning leadership in a self-managed team, he or she should "always" work hard to facilitate idea generation and innovation, help define and champion overall goals, search for conceptual links between systems, and foster frame-breaking thinking. Intensity is the high level of energy and commitment on the part of individual team members. In a self-managed team, individual commitment to team tasks and group processes, in particular, is a necessary guarantee to the effective functioning of the "leaderless" team. Permanent dissatisfaction comes from a high level of energy and commitment and demonstrates itself in the individual members' continuous effort to excel. Speedy and effective communication is probably the most important factor weighing on the success of a self-managed team with the absence of formal authority; this not only facilitates task-related information sharing but also helps promote group development processes. A self-managed team, when it meets the criteria of consistency, intensity, permanent dissatisfaction, and speedy and effective communication, will be able to generate high-speed management teamwork.

Executive-Level Teamwork

The emergence of teamwork at the top of an organization represents another response to the high-speed management environment characterized externally by a volatile business market and internally by the complexity of production. Ancona and Nadler (1989) argue that three factors account for the necessity of executive-level teamwork: external demands, organizational complexity, and succession. External business pressures have played a major role. "Increasing global competition, technology-based change, and turbulence in financial markets all add to the burdens of the CEO. In addition, the need to spend more time on strate-

FIGURE 4.2
A Model of Executive Team Effectiveness

Team Design	Core Management	Team Performance
Composition	Work Management	Production of "Results"
Structure	Relationship Management	
Succession	External Boundary Management	Maintenance of Effectiveness

Source: Ancona and Nadler 1989, p. 23.

gies to meet environmental instability must be balanced with a focus on short-term performance, driven by shareholder demands and concerns about takeover. As a consequence, CEOs are more often looking for strategic and operational help" (p. 21). In the old CEO/COO executive structural model, the CEO is responsible for strategic issues, external relations, and overall corporate governance, while the COO takes care of internal operations. The two-person CEO/COO structure is still the dominant leadership form, but the team model is gaining acceptance and popularity.

To present an executive-level teamwork model in the context of high-speed management, we wish to add the four high-speed management teamwork qualities of consistency, intensity, permanent dissatisfaction, and speedy and effective communication to Ancona and Nadler's model of executive team effectiveness. Figure 4.2 depicts the Ancona and Nadler model:

Team Design Team design contains elements that are determined before core processes are set in motion. In terms of *composition*, the selection of team members should be based on whether s/he has skills and experiences on the one hand and favorable personality qualities on the other. *Team structure* is defined by the nature of team positions (business unit heads as opposed to functional leaders), the size of the team, the boundaries (who's in and out), the specific formal roles, the goals, and the nature of team and individual rewards. *Succession* is the third design element that is crucial for the organizational and leadership stability and continuity. To the three elements of team design as suggested by Ancona and Nadler, we may add the quality of intensity. The high level of energy and commitment should certainly be required of all the members of the executive team, including the CEO. The quality of *intensity* should be used as a major criterion with which to select team members, determine who is in and who is out, and assess the succession issue.

Core Processes The Ancona and Nadler model includes three core processes: work management, relationship management, and external boundary management. *Work management process* is a process in which the team makes and implements decisions regarding strategies, policy issues, and routine task operations. *Relationship management process* involves the degree of openness between members, how conflicts are resolved, the nature of support expressed among members, the cohesiveness of the group, and the level of trust. *External boundary management process* is one by which team members deal with factors outside the organizational boundary such as financial markets, the media, key customers, competitors, and governments. The process could also include the managing of the boundary between the top team and the rest of the organization. For the three core management processes to qualify as high-speed management teamwork processes, we may add the quality of *speedy and effective communication*. We believe that speedy and effective communication is the only process tool that the executive-level team can use to meet the challenges from the work management, relationship management, and external boundary management in the context of high-speed management.

Team Performance Team performance is twofold. One side is the production of results, which includes the quality of decision making, the ability to implement decisions, the outcomes of teamwork in terms of problems solved and work completed, and the quality of institutional leadership provided. The other side is the maintenance of effectiveness, which refers to the team's ability to maintain an esprit de corps and quality team climate characterized by a high level of mutual trust and support. It seems that another high-speed teamwork quality—*permanent dissatisfaction*—should fit here. When the team members feel permanently dissatisfied with team performance, the sustaining competitive edge of the organization can then be ensured.

The remaining high-speed management teamwork quality of *consistency* should be present all through the teamwork process of an executive-level team, from team design, through core processes, to team performance. With the four high-speed management teamwork qualities of consistency, intensity, speedy and effective communication, and permanent dissatisfaction added to Ancona and Nadler's model of executive team effectiveness, we have a model that would fit in the high-speed management context (figure 4.3).

Social-Technical Teamwork

It has been more than thirty years since the first article on social-technical systems, based on field work done in coal mines in Great Britain, was published (Emery and Trist 1960). The recent enthusiasm in the sociotechnical philosophy has been kindled by a high-speed management environment where, as Kolodny and Dresner point out when they are writing on the philosophy, "the high levels of global competitiveness, galloping technological change, and customer and client demands for increased responsiveness have made flexibility in production processes and rapid product throughput highly desirable" (Kolodny and Dresner 1986, p. 35). Such flexibility demands both a most efficient and effective production process (technical) and an adaptive work force (social) at the same time. Social-technical teams are designed to meet the two demands of flexibility.

FIGURE 4.3
A Model of Executive Team Effectiveness

Team Design	Core Management	Team Performance
Composition	Work Management	Production of "Results"
Structure	Relationship Management	
Succession	External Boundary Management	Maintenance of Effectiveness

Intensity	*Speedy and Effective Communication*	*Permanent Dissatisfaction*

Typically, the formation of social-technical teamwork is based on two kinds of analysis, technical analysis and social analysis (Taylor and Asadorian 1985). Technical analysis is made on unit operations, key factors, and variance control, while social analysis includes evaluation of functional relationships and requirements examination, focal role network, and quality of working life. The key to the success of social-technical teamwork is the organizational effort to achieve "joint optimization" of both the technical system and social system (Kolodny and Dresner 1986; Taylor and Asadorian 1985).

Technical Analysis The first step of technical analysis is the identification of unit operations. A *unit operation* is defined as a meaningful transformation of an input into an output within a technical process. Technology is defined in terms of its input and product, instead of by its tools, processes, or techniques. This focus, according to Taylor and Asadorian (1985), ensures that the technical system will be analyzed separately from the jobs and work of people, on the one hand, and from the supervisory and control system, on the other. Identification of *key factors* represents the second step of technical analysis. This is done through three substeps. First, all the technical factors (aspects and conditions) involved in each unit operation are listed. Second, those factors that have a direct or important impact on quantity, quality, or costs of the system output are singled out for detailed examination. Third, a *Key Factor Identification Chart* is drawn and probably posted on the wall so that production operators are kept aware of those factors and possible variances. *Variance control* is the step that actually forms a bridge between the technical process and social process. Some of the crucial questions to be asked regarding variance control may include, for example, where and how the variances have originated, who controls the key variance, and how it is controlled. Variances are much better controlled by production operators—people on the front line—who keep a high level of energy and commitment, and are capable of speedy and effective communication.

Social Analysis An organization is also a social system that, in the context of high-speed management, is "the co-ordinating and integrating buffer between the technical transformation process and the demands and constraints of a turbulent environment" (Taylor and Asadorian 1985, p. 11). According to Taylor and Asadorian

(1985), in order to survive in a turbulent environment, an organization as a social system must perform four basic functions:

1. setting and attaining performance goals (G)
2. adapting to the external environment (A)
3. integrating the activities of people within the system (I)
4. seeking long-term development (L)

The analysis of the four functional requirements (G, A, I, L) must be combined with the particular functional relationships (vertical, horizontal, internal, cross boundary relationships) that affect the satisfaction of the requirements. This combination is charted in a 4 × 4 *social system grid*. Social analysis also involves the examination of the roles and relationships within the whole work process, with the focus on the roles that are crucial in the control of key variances. This is *focal role analysis*. The patterns of interaction (communication) can be mapped in terms of frequency and direction of contact. The third step in the social analysis is the evaluation of *quality of working life*. This is to assess how workers' individual needs, both material and psychological, are satisfied. This step is crucial in the sense that failure to ensure the quality of working life may threaten the very success of social-technical teamwork.

As we pointed out earlier, the key to the functioning of social-technical teamwork is the *joint optimization* of both the technical system and social system. This not only suggests that the technical analysis and social analysis in the initial system design should be conducted simultaneously but also invites the introduction of the four high-speed management teamwork qualities, namely, consistency, intensity, permanent dissatisfaction, and speedy and effective communication. When the four qualities are added to the conventional social-technical teamwork model, it will fit in a much better way into the high-speed management context. While the four qualities should apply to the overall social-technical teamwork process, it seems that the qualities of intensity and permanent dissatisfaction are more closely related to the variance control system in the technical analysis, and the quality of speedy and effective communication may have a direct bearing on the focal role networking in the social analysis. The quality of consistency, as with the other teamwork patterns, should be present throughout the social-technical process.

Having discussed the four teamwork patterns—cross-functional, self-managed, executive-level and social-technical—in the high-speed management context, we are now in a position to take a look at two world leaders that have been following high-speed management principles and have benefited greatly from teamwork: Toyota Motor Company in Japan and GE in the United States. Instead of using the four patterns to examine their teamwork in a mechanical way (even though all these patterns have effectively been followed there), we will try to highlight those aspects that characterize the two industrial giants' success stories of how teamwork is used to get the job done. However, the four high-speed management teamwork criteria of consistency, intensity, permanent dissatisfaction, and speedy and effective communication will, again, be called in as tools to help with our evaluation and reinforce the theme of this chapter.

TEAMWORK AT TOYOTA MOTOR COMPANY

Toyota is the best carmaker in the world. And it keeps getting "better and better and better." Japan's number one automaker, jokingly known as the "Bank of Toyota," is so rich that it now sits on $22 billion in cash—enough to buy both Ford and Chrysler at current stock prices, with nearly $5 billion to spare (Taylor 1990, pp. 68–69). Why "better and better and better"? And why doing so well financially in a time when the Big Three in the United States seem to be in serious trouble? Different theories may be developed to explain the Toyota success story, but teamwork is our explanation. While the result of teamwork is certainly positive, we will focus on how it is carried out and, probably more importantly, why the way it is carried out is possible. Given the limited space of the chapter, our discussion offers no more than a brief look at the teamwork on Toyota's production line and the company's coalignment with its suppliers and dealers/customers outside the organizational boundary.

Teamwork on the Production Line

The main philosophy that underlines the whole production system is *efficiency and cost reduction*. The key to achieving efficiency and cost reduction is, understandably, the workers, men and women of the Toyota family who are required to "be contributive to the development and welfare of the country by working together, regardless of position, in faithfully fulfilling your duties; be at the vanguard of the times through endless creativity, inquisitiveness and pursuit of improvement; be practical and avoid frivolity; be kind and generous, strive to create a warm, homelike atmosphere; be reverent, and show gratitude for things great and small in thought and deed" (Toyoda 1988, pp. 37–38). These company admonitions may all be called "teamwork principles." Translating these principles into realities at the very beginning of the work process: hiring team-conscious people. Once they are hired, they will have lifetime employment. The company has been trying hard to enrich assembly-line jobs, by making the work more creative, and to make them safer, by eliminating three Ds: the dangerous, dirty, and demanding aspects of factory work (Taylor 1990).

In order to attain efficiency and cost reduction in the whole production system, Toyota uses four management concepts—just-in-time, autonomation, flexibility, and creative thinking—the realization of which depends very much on teamwork. Therefore these four management concepts can also be called "teamwork ideas."

Just-in-Time As the name suggests, this concept emphasizes a production system that cuts back on surplus stock and keeps on hand only essential materials for a preset production tempo. Just-in-time increases efficiency and decreases capital outflow (Toyoda 1988). To make just-in-time work, *kanban* is used. *Kanban* is an information system that transmits information to the preceding process and indicates what the current process needs. A *kanban* is a card. There are two kinds of such cards: withdrawal *kanban* and production-ordering *kanban*. A withdrawal *kanban* specifies the kind and quantity of product that the subsequent process should withdraw from the preceding process. A production-ordering *kanban* specifies the kind and quantity of the product that the preceding process must produce (Fischetti 1987, pp. 50–52). Just-in-time obviously puts pressure on workers and demands teamwork that realizes coalignment between the preceding process and subsequent process. *Speedy and effective communication* is particularly important in making the *kanban* system work in a smooth and noninterrupting way.

Autonomation This refers to how man and machine cooperate to control defects. The Toyota production line is designed in such a way that whenever a defect is detected by a mechanical system or a worker, the line can be stopped. This introduces the idea of *kaizen*, which means "continuous improvement" in Japanese. *Kaizen* translates into "zero defect" on the production line and relates nicely to a more popular management tool called the "quality control circle," which is based on worker initiatives and their willingness to improve. *Kaizen* puts responsibility on the workers and "responsibility means freedom to control one's job" (Womack, Jones, and Roos 1990a, p. 38). Toyota workers' freedom to stop the production line, for example, demands not only that they command superior production skills, which enable them to detect errors, but that they be highly responsible and committed to what they are assigned to work on. "In Toyota plants, where every worker can halt the line, yields approach 100 percent, and the line practically never stops" (p. 38). It seems that here the high-speed management teamwork qualities of *intensity* and *permanent dissatisfaction* are particularly relevant to the success of autonomation.

Flexibility A flexible workforce is realized through a proper design of machinery layout, well-trained multifunction workers, and continuous evaluation and periodic revisions of the standard operations routine. At Toyota, machines are set up in a U-turn layout instead of the traditional straight-line design. The U-turn layout not only helps in meeting production demands but also encourages team spirit that is so much a part of the production system. Multifunction workers are capable of handling various machines. When one process is complete, s/he may move on to a different machine to perform an entirely different task. The U-turn machine layout helps workers make the switch from one machine to another in an easy and efficient way. Standard operations allow for a balance of production with minimum labor. High productivity is achieved through "strenuous work," which is defined as working efficiently without wasteful motions (Hochi 1986, pp. 24–29). As is implied in the process, teamwork, as opposed to individual task-orientation, is emphasized. Here again the teamwork qualities of *intensity* and *permanent dissatisfaction* should be present to allow a workforce to be flexible.

Creative Thinking This refers to how to capitalize on the ideas and suggestions of the worker. Through involvement in such team activities as the quality control circle, workers are encouraged to be active participants in creating improvements in all aspects in the workplace. It seems that workers' *permanent dissatisfaction* in an increasingly tough business environment adds to the sustaining competitive advantage of the Toyota Motor Company. A year-by-year comparison of how Toyota workers' involvement in creative activities in the company (table 4.1):

Having discussed briefly the four teamwork based management concepts at Toyota and qualified each of them with one or two of the four high-speed management teamwork qualities, we wish to add that the quality of *consistency* has always been present in the whole production process, and that is why "Toyota is getting better and better and better." We also want to point out that the principle of *consistency* applies equally well in its team-

TABLE 4.1
Employees Suggestion Systems at Toyota

FY	Suggestions	Adopted %	Suggestions per Worker
1951	789	23	0.1
1955	1,087	53	0.2
1960	5,001	33	0.6
1965	15,968	39	0.7
1969	40,313	68	1.1
1970	49,414	72	1.3
1971	88,607	74	2.2
1972	168,458	75	4.1
1973	284,717	77	6.7
1974	398,091	78	9.0
1975	381,438	83	8.5
1976	463,422	84	10.4
1977	454,522	84	10.2
1978	527,861	88	11.7
1979	575,861	91	12.7
1980	859,039	94	18.6
1981	1,412,565	94	29.5
1982	1,905,642	95	32.7
1983	1,655,858	96	28.2

Source: Adapted from Cusumano, pp. 358–59.

work with the relevant environment outside the boundary of the Toyota Motor Company. Our next task is now to examine how Toyota manages its interorganizational teamwork, and our focus will be on its teamwork with its suppliers and dealers/customers, the two end subsystems outside the organizational structure as shown in the organizational value chain discussed earlier in this chapter.

Interorganizational Teamwork with Suppliers and Dealers/Customers

Suppliers represent the starting point of the organizational value chain. As early as in the 1950s, Toyota divided its suppliers into separate tiers with different responsibilities. First-tier suppliers were each assigned a major component such as car seats or the electrical system. Second-tier suppliers would supply individual parts or subsystem components to the first-tier companies. Second-tier suppliers, in many cases, developed a third-level of suppliers that supplied what the former needed. Toyota only dealt with the first-tier suppliers. These companies became an integral part of the product-development team and were well informed of a car model's performance specifications.

Teamwork between Toyota and its first-tier suppliers is possible as both expect the relationship to be a long-term and stable one. In the spirit of teamwork, Toyota is provided with the most sensitive information about the suppliers' operations, including costs and quality levels. Information sharing also occurs at meetings of first-tier and second-tier supplier associations, where advances in manufacturing techniques are discussed. As a rule, Toyota design engineers visit first-tier plants to observe and take part in the production planning for the new model. One of the most impressive aspects of the supply system is, again, just-in-time. Thanks to the cooperation between the assembler and supplier, practically all inventories are eliminated, further lowering the overall manufacturing cost of a car.

Toyota also has a very close relationship with its dealers/customers. Its distribution function is divided among a number of nationwide channels, each of which sells a portion of the company's product range. One of Toyota's channels, Corolla, for example, sells its cars through seventy-eight dealer firms. The channel owns 20 percent of the dealerships. The 30,400 employees of the channel sell about 635,000 cars and trucks a year. At each Corolla dealership, the sales staff is organized into teams of seven or eight people who are trained in all aspects of the job. Team meetings are held on a daily basis. When sales drop to the point where the factory no longer has enough orders to sustain full output, production personnel are transferred into the sales system (Womack, Jones, and Roos 1990, p. 22). This shows that the production system of the factory and the sales people at the dealerships are so well coaligned that they become one larger team.

Speedy and effective communication is crucial to maintaining high-level teamwork between the factory and the dealerships. Sales team members draw up a profile of every household within the geographic area around the dealership and make periodic visits to update the profile: how many cars of what age that each family has; what makes of car with what features; the number of children in the household; the uses of cars in a household; when the family thinks it needs to replace its cars. Such information, together with sales people's suggestions regarding the most appropriate specifications for a new vehicle, is speedily sent to the production system of the factory. And these suggestions are carefully studied for clues to changing customer tastes. At the factory, executives determine how different models, colors, and the like will sell; then they establish a production schedule. The objective is to get the right combination going down the line to match actual demand. The production schedule is frequently revised as the dealers gather and communicate customer feedback. Corrections and adjustments are made quickly, and so the right cars speedily go to the right customers! Thanks to the close coalignment between the production system and the dealerships/customers, the whole distribution network contains an average of just three weeks' supply of finished units, compared to two months' supply in the United States (Womack, Jones, and Roos 1990a). Obviously, interorganizational teamwork gives another reason why Toyota "keeps getting better and better and better."

TEAMWORK AT GE

General Electric is one of the largest and best run companies in the United States and in the world. Since legendary Jack Welch took office in the early 1980s, 115-year old GE, in its drive to become leaner and more competitive, has slashed more than one hundred thousand jobs worldwide and kept only those businesses that rank either number one or number two worldwide or domestically. Each of its remaining thirteen businesses has annual revenues from $2.5 billion to $13 billion. During a five-year period ending in 1990, GE doubled revenues and net income to $55 billion and $4 billion, respectively (Quickel 1990, pp. 64, 62). Interestingly, although the conceptual labels that GE has been using as management tools appear to be quite different from those of Toyota, they are, in essence, as much teamwork oriented as the Japanese company's management concepts. Briefly, we will discuss the following teamwork ideas that Jack Welch and GE have been promoting in recent years, ideas that have translated into tremendous human energies and billions of dollars: boundarylessness; integrated diversity; Work-Out; and Best Practices Studies.

Boundarylessness

Jack Welch's newest philosophy of management is to create a "boundaryless company." "In a boundaryless company," according to Welch, "internal functions begin to blur. Engineering doesn't design a product and then 'hand it off' to manufacturing. They form a team, along with marketing and sales, finance and the rest" (Annual Report of GE 1990). Therefore, to create a boundaryless company, arbitrary divisions between all parts of the value chain, from supplier to company to dealer/customer, are blurred or eliminated. The cross-functional teamwork which characterizes a boundaryless organization allows a faster flow of information, a more participative decision-making process, and speedy corrections and adjustments. The philosophy of boundarylessness, as it spreads in GE, reminds us of Toyota's teamwork both at the organizational and interorganizational levels.

Integrated Diversity

"Integrated diversity" is another buzz phrase that "peppers Welch's conversations these days" (Quickel 1990, p. 66). While it could mean almost the same thing as boundarylessness, it is mainly concerned with how GE's thirteen businesses should help each other, as opposed to operating as separate fiefdoms. Welch explains: "Most diversified companies do a good job of transferring technical resources and dollars across their businesses. A few do a good job of transferring human resources effectively. We think we do the best job of transferring management practices across our businesses—the best techniques, the best systems ideas, the best generic growth and superior profitability" (p. 66). What needs to be pointed out is the fact that GE's thirteen diversified businesses, each one an independently run, large, and complex organization, are scattered around the world. The realization of integrated diversity represents major efforts on the part of each business to manage interorganizational teamwork at the global level.

Work-Out

This is probably the best known teamwork concept that Jack Welch has created, and he describes Work-Out as the ultimate boundaryless event. Welch was determined to engage the hearts and minds of GE's 291,000 worldwide employees from the top managers of the thirteen multibillion-dollar businesses down to the factory floor. This is realized through Work-Out—a program of ongoing, company-wide town meetings where employees at all levels are encouraged to chip in ideas to make GE more competitive (Quickel 1990, p. 62). Every week throughout GE, groups of 50 to 150 employees gather in two- or three-day Work-Out sessions. Work-Out sessions are attended by employees picked from all levels, often for their expertise and involvement in the business issues slated for primary discussion. About twenty thousand to twenty-five thousand GE employees attend Work-Out sessions each year. Work-Out corresponds nicely to Toyota's practice of the quality control circle. The difference between the two seems to be that while the Work-Out process is more top-down and encourages employees to "speak out," quality control circle activities tend to occur more on a voluntary basis. The goal is the same: *kaizen* or continuous improvement in an increasingly volatile and competitive high-speed management environment.

Best Practice Studies

The Best Practices Studies program was initiated shortly after Work-Out was introduced in GE. The program aims at discovering world benchmark processes, practices, and quality standards through a cooperative learning relationship with those companies holding the standard. Through in-depth studies of these best practices, sometimes involving personnel from an outside organization working together with GE personnel (in exchange for an opportunity to study GE's best practices), these international benchmark standards are absorbed into GE's practices and processes. About two years ago, GE completed a series of Best Practices Studies to examine the management techniques of ten world-class companies ranging from AMP and Xerox to Chaparral Steel and Japan's Honda. All ten companies accepted GE's request to study their best practices, in return for a similar detailed inside look at GE's management methods. Obviously, the Best Practices Studies program relates nicely, again, to the idea of interorganizational teamwork. To be informed of the world benchmark standards seems to be crucial for each of GE's thirteen remaining businesses to stay number one or number two.

A careful reading of Jack Welch's four management/teamwork concepts will easily lead to the conclusion that the four high-speed management teamwork criteria of consistency, intensity, permanent dissatisfaction, and speedy and effective communication appear to be best followed in the ongoing process of creating a boundaryless company—in the generation of integrated diversity, in Work-Out town meetings, and in Best Practices Studies.

MODEL OF TEAMWORK IN THE CONTEXT OF HIGH-SPEED MANAGEMENT

A crucial question we may ask after examining the teamwork concepts at two of the world's most successful companies is, What can we learn from Toyota and GE? Is it that all companies need to follow suit, generating programs identical or similar to "just-in-time," "autonomation," "flexibility," and "creative thinking" at Toyota or creating "a boundaryless company," "integrated diversity," "Work-Out," and "Best Practices Studies" as GE did? The answer is no. Every organization may well develop its own management programs and teamwork patterns, since each has its own particularities to deal with. Nothing is worse than mere copying in an increasingly competitive high tech age. Just-in-time just works well at Toyota, but not necessarily at GE. And Work-Out works beautifully at GE, but probably not at Toyota. However, we do believe, on the basis of our discussion on teamwork at Toyota and GE, that the two companies share some fundamental high-speed management teamwork philosophies, and these proven philosophies should be dealt with seriously. We present six fundamental high-speed management teamwork philosophies shared by Toyota and GE and all other organizations that have performed well in the high-speed environment:

First, teamwork should be a goal-driven process, and the general goal of teamwork in the context of high-speed management is speed-to-market and quality. Talking about teamwork without an articulation of some achievable goals and talking about high-speed management teamwork without having "speed-to-market" and "quality" in mind are like talking about managerial gimmicks.

Second, the context of high-speed management presupposes the need for interorganizational teamwork as well as intraorganizational teamwork. Toyota's teamwork with its suppliers and dealers/customers and GEs management's integrated diversity and Best Practices Studies are examples of fulfilling such a need. The globalization of economic systems and intensification of international trade require firms and companies to manage well their inter- as well as intraorganizational interdependencies.

Third, there will be no teamwork without the commitment of team members, and highly committed team members are an ultimate guarantee of teamwork in the high-speed management context. Commitment on the part of team members generates and maintains team spirit, and high commitment leads to high team spirit. This equals the idea of "intensity," one of the four high-speed management teamwork qualities we use as the focal theme of this chapter.

Fourth, teamwork in the context of high-speed management is characterized by team members' permanent dissatisfaction with products and services. Toyota's *kaizen* and quality control circle, and GE's Work-Out and Best Practices Studies offer examples of such spirit.

Fifth, teamwork in the context of high-speed management follows speedy and effective communication. The essence of high-speed management is high-speed communication, high-speed sharing of information, high-speed problem-solving, and ultimately high speed to the market. Communication in high-speed management teams must be speedier and more effective not only because teams need to solve problems quickly but also because the problems that need to be solved tend to be more complicated—much more complicated in some cases—than they are in a non-high-speed environment.

Sixth, teamwork in the context of high-speed management must consistently be of high quality. As we pointed out earlier in the chapter, teamwork is a condition; it can come and go. Toyota keeps getting better and better and better, and GE is becoming increasingly competitive in the world economy, simply because they have been consistent in their teamwork approach all along.

We combine the six philosophies to form our model of teamwork in the context of high-speed management (figure 4.4).

This model consists of three clusters of elements: functional elements, structural elements, and qualitative elements. Functional elements include "speed-to-market" and "quality," which combine to suggest that teamwork is a goal driven process. Structural elements belong to two main groups, intraorganizational teamwork, which occurs along all system parts of the value chain, and interorganizational teamwork, which co-aligns with organizations outside the structure of an organization; they find themselves at either end of the value chain. Qualitative elements are the four qualities of intensity, permanent dissatisfaction, speedy and effective communication, and consistency. This is both a descriptive and prescriptive model, the vigor and usefulness of which is yet to be tested.

FIGURE 4.4
Model of Teamwork in the Context of High-Speed Management

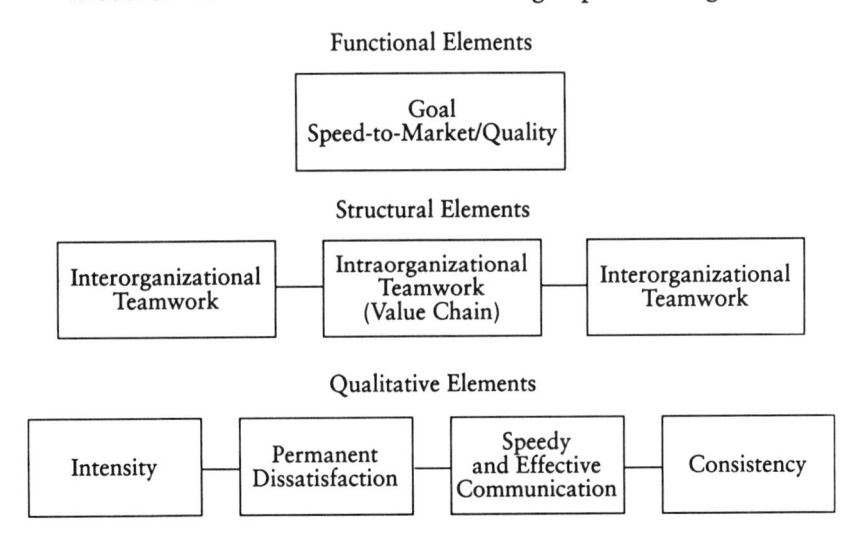

Functional Elements

Goal
Speed-to-Market/Quality

Structural Elements

Interorganizational Teamwork — Intraorganizational Teamwork (Value Chain) — Interorganizational Teamwork

Qualitative Elements

Intensity — Permanent Dissatisfaction — Speedy and Effective Communication — Consistency

CHAPTER 5

Organizational Structure: A Killer or Facilitator of Teamwork

> Structure kills. Most are moving to reduce it. Few are moving fast enough. Excess middle management staff—often to the tune of several hundred percent—still exists in most big firms and even in many smaller and midsized firms.
>
> Today's structures were designed for controlling turn-of-the-century mass-production operations under stable conditions, with primitive technologies. They have become perverse, action-destroying devices, completely at odds with current competitive needs.
>
> T. Peters, *Thriving on Chaos*

Teamwork is a process in which team players cross functional boundaries to work together on some task or project, a process where organizational hierarchy, rules and regulations, and strict role definitions are defied in order to get the job done faster to meet the market needs better. Teamwork, thus defined, collides head-on with an organization's traditional structure characterized by multiple layers of management, rigidly defined functional, product, and/or geographical lines, and often an awesome number of rules and regulations. Teamwork, as it is becoming increasingly popular with firms, is a direct organizational response to an increasingly competitive environment that is characterized by rapid technological change, shortened product life cycles, quick market saturation, and unexpected competition. Such an environment has demanded that traditional organizational structure be changed so that it will be capable of assisting an innovative, adaptive, flexible, efficient, and rapid response management. How fast and how thorough this structural change is would very much affect how successfully teamwork can be conducted in an organization.

In this chapter, we will first explain why paradigm shifting is necessary before an organization is committed to making radical changes, including structural changes. This is followed by an examination of how an over-layered hierarchy should be replaced by a simplified, responsive structure, how bureaucratic rules and regulations should be slashed and then melted into the culture, and how rigid managerial/worker role definitions should become so fluid that a horizontal movement across functional boundaries will be not only possible but also easy. We will then take a look at how the flexibly structured "adaptive organization" actually works with its very much simplified and reduced structure. We will end the chapter with a brief discussion on the almost-no-structure "virtual organization," which emphasizes teamwork among strategic alliances.

PARADIGM SHIFTING TO WAKE UP THE DYING FROG

Noel Tichy adapted the boiled frog experiment from the biology lab to management theory. The frog experiment is simple: If you put a frog in a pot of boiling water, the little thing will jump right out. But if you place it in a pot of cold water and gradually raise the temperature of the water, it will sit there and boil to death. Jack Welch of GE notes that in industry after industry, a lot of frogs are waking up and finding it's too late to jump.

Traditional organizational structure has a numbing effect on firms, making them insensitive to the heat that is building up in the environment. When an organization has been in a structure for too long and has been doing business the same way for too long, it will resist change, and radical change in particular. Unfortunately, many such organizations have boiled to death without realizing that they were dying just like the frog in the experiment lab.

To avoid the fate of a boiled frog, firms, big and small, must introduce what is called "paradigm shifting," a kind of change that could be so fundamental and radical that the dying frog would suddenly wake up and jump out of the killing pot. Huey (1991) writes that a paradigm, in its business connotation, is simply the conventional wisdom about how things have always been done and must continue to be done. *A paradigm shifter is one who throws out old rules of the game and institutes radical change, a leader who foments revolution, not evolution.* Paradigm shifting is never easy, and oftentimes involves the great risk of the paradigm shifter being eliminated by conservative forces. Huey (1991) reports that real paradigm shifting rarely occurs within traditional corporations. When it does, individual paradigm shifters who attempt to rock the corporate boat often don't survive the process.

Individual paradigm shifters don't survive the process because the resisting forces can be so overwhelming that they will all jump on them and strangle them to death. How can people not jump on those who are, for example, slashing two layers of management, closing down a whole functional department, trying to execute a massive managerial layoff plan? Isn't there a life and death struggle between the paradigm shifter and resisting forces? Therefore it takes moral courage, tenacity, and corporate support from the very top to introduce any radical structural change. Whatever the cost, this must be done to wake up the dying frog, or everybody dies together with it.

AN OVER-LAYERED HIERARCHY VERSUS A SIMPLIFIED, RESPONSIVE STRUCTURE

Peters writes: "Peter Drucker in his classic book *The Practice of Management* recommends seven layers as the maximum necessary for any organization. But that was in 1954, a more placid era. I insist on five layers as the maximum. Incidentally, that's the number of layers with which the Catholic Church makes do to oversee 800 million members. As Eli Ginzberg and George Vojta observe in *Beyond Human Scale: The large Corporations at Risk*: ' Many writers on organization have termed the Catholic Church the most venerable large institution in the West, as it has achieved and maintained a position of leadership and power for over a millennium and a half. A key organizational characteristic of the Church is that despite its size it has avoided excessive layering'" (Peters 1987, p. 430) Peters immediately adds that his five-layer suggestion should apply only to very complex organizations. For any single facility such as a plant or distribution center, he says, three layers, which include supervisor, department head, and unit boss, are sufficient.

Whether the magic number is seven or five or three is not the point. The point is that an over-layered structure must be simplified and reduced because it kills speed and responsiveness to market needs and thus a firm's competitive advantage. Understandably, a lot of fat that needs to be cut lies in the middle management, and that is exactly what is being taken care of in many speed- and responsiveness-conscious organizations. Dumaine (1993) reports that the American Management Association says that while middle managers compose only about 5 percent of the work force at the 836 companies it surveyed, they account for 22 percent of 1992's layoffs. The massive layoffs seem to be justified by the seemingly permanent loss of the middle manager's two main functions: supervising people and gathering, processing, and transmitting information. The disappearance of the job of supervising people has very much been caused by the forming of cross-functional or self-managing teams, which are taking over such standard supervisory duties as scheduling work, maintaining quality, and administering pay and vacations. And the wide availability and user friendliness of computers and other information technologies have granted ordinary workers the capability of handling information on their own, which logically causes the loss of the supervisor's information processing job. What seems favorable to the process of teamwork is quite an unhappy experience for a traditional middle manager.

As it has been exposed to constant environmental challenge, an over-layered organizational structure seems to have shown the following inherent ills:

1. An over-layered structure inherently resists the very idea of teamwork, since it tends to be perceived as a threat to the legitimacy of at least some layers. Such a structure has a built-in tendency to block or delay a smooth horizontal movement of personnel across various functional lines. Any attempt to move across a functional line or form a cross functional or self-managing team can invite resentment or resistance from the hierarchy. And that is why, as we suggested in the first section of this chapter, paradigm shifting is necessary to clear the road of resistance before teams can be formed and function in a healthy way.

2. An over-layered structure complicates the reporting relationships among individual team members on the one hand and between the team leader and head of that leader's original functional unit on the other. Wherever possible, the traditional hierarchy enjoys having team players report back to their original functional heads, and this can negatively impact the normal functioning of a team.

3. An over-layered structure discourages or even prevents information-sharing among team members, because the disclosure of any critical information that a manager of a particular layer used to have the privilege to hold could threaten the very stability of his or her bureaucratic position.

4. An over-layered structure creates barriers to the execution of a strategic plan or major conclusion that a team has made as a result of the teamwork, thus delaying response to a competitive need.

It seems clear that an over-layered structure runs counter to the very idea of teamwork and high-speed management. *To facilitate teamwork and the carrying out of high-speed management premises, a firm faced with an unstable environment must replace its over-layered structure with something simplified and responsive.* Before any concrete measure can be taken, one must first of all change the framework within which one used to think. One such framework is the organization chart. Traditionally, people have always thought that on top of the organization chart should sit the top management, at middle layers, the middle management; and then at the bottom of the pyramid, front-line workers, called the "managed." As implied in the physical appearance of the traditional organization chart, the higher up in the hierarchy, the more important one was likely to be perceived. The least important were always the front-line workers. To change the way of thinking about who is more important and who is less so in an organization, we need to reverse the pyramid by putting those who used to be at the bottom at the top, and those who used to be at the top at the bottom. Organizing the line workers into various teams and seeing managers and staff as support people produces a reversed chart (fig. 5.1). This chart consists of three layers, with the top at the bottom and the bottom at the top. Notice that we do not even see "managers," who have been replaced by so-called coaches and facilitators. In some less complex organizations, the middle layer and the top layer can well be merged into one. It is not entirely unthinkable to have a structure with only two layers (fig. 5.2). Some paradigm shifters may even want to go a step further by eliminating the whole hierarchy (fig. 5.3).

This last alternative may drive insane some hard-core lovers of traditional organizational hierarchy. So let's put it aside for a moment and stick with the first and second reversed charts. Some

FIGURE 5.1
A Three-Layer Reversed Pyramid

Front-Line Workers or Team Members

Mid-Level Coaches or Facilitators

Top-Level Coaches or Facilitators

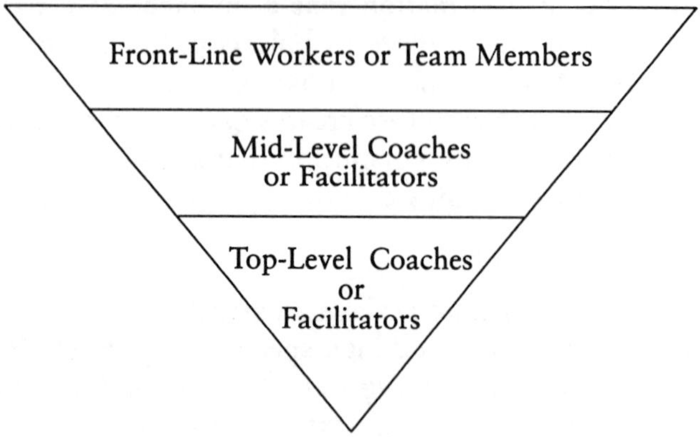

FIGURE 5.2
A Two-Layer Reversed Pyramid

Front-Line Workers or Team Members

Coaches or Facilitators

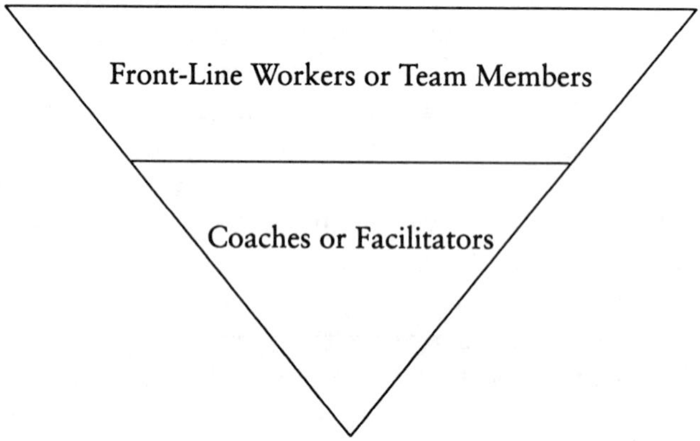

FIGURE 5.3
A Hierarchy-Free Structure

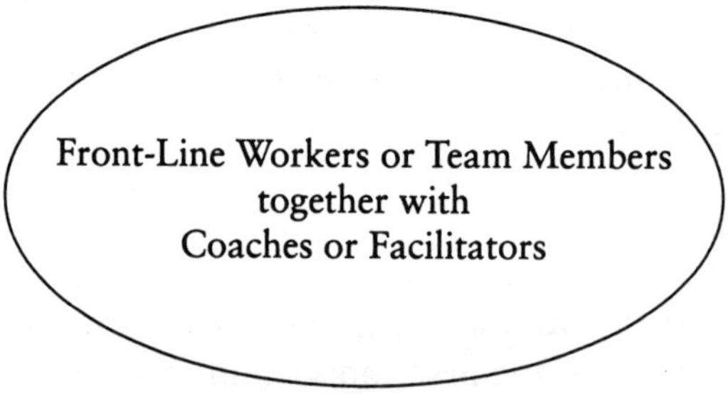

Front-Line Workers or Team Members
together with
Coaches or Facilitators

common characteristics may be identified with these two reversed charts:

1. They look much leaner and simpler than a traditional organizational hierarchy.
2. They both put front-line workers or team players in the most important position in the sense they are now closest to the customers or the external environment, thus greatly increasing a firm's responsiveness to market needs.
3. They both redefine the role of management. They see managers, top or middle, more as coaches or facilitators whose job is to help front-line workers or team members to solve problems.
4. In a nonhierarchical environment, communication takes place more easily between and among team members and their coaches/facilitators, hence there can be quicker decision making and more timely response to market needs.

Less is more, and a lot less is a lot more. Peters concludes: "Pruning central staff/layers by 50 to 90 percent leads to more responsiveness and better staff work. It all adds up to this: If you have more than a handful of people at headquarters, if you have more than a few layers, you are in trouble—or fast heading for it. It's as simple and stark as that" (Peters 1987, p. 434).

MELTING RULES AND REGULATIONS INTO TEAM CULTURE

An over-layered hierarchy is always matched with high stacks of bureaucratic rules and regulations, the inventing and executing of which seems to be the very job of managers. Therefore, reducing bureaucratic rules and regulations is as difficult as slashing excessive layers of management. In the same token, when an organization's structure is flattened, its bureaucratic rules and regulations must also be abandoned.

Bureaucratic rules and regulations are another dead enemy of organizational teamwork and high-speed management. By nature, rules and regulations—here we refer to those that are written on the paper or posted on the wall—tend to slow action or even prevent it from happening. Peters asked, "Have you ever heard of anyone going to a rule book to figure out how to speed things up?"

We are not advocating a complete elimination of rules and regulations; indeed no organization can function in an orderly way without enforcing certain rules and regulations. Here we are suggesting that after probably two-thirds of an organization's existing rules and regulations are gotten rid of, the majority of the remaining one-third be transformed into the organization's culture. *When a certain rule gets deeply rooted in an organization member's psychology and behavior pattern, its original bureaucratic nature will be negated and it will become something very practical and useful.* Here we are suggesting that a positive team culture be nurtured, a culture which is built on what may be called the "three golden values" as they have been paid homage to in Ouchi's Theory Z (Ouchi 1981). These are the values of trust, subtlety, and intimacy. They could be more powerful than ten thousand rules and regulations.

Trust, subtlety, and intimacy generate action, productivity, and above all, speed, which is so crucial in high-speed management. And they, much more than rules and regulations, are the real guarantee of the smooth functioning of teamwork. Ouchi believed that these were the lessons that American firms should learn from their Japanese counterparts, adding that they could be universally applicable. It has already been more than a decade since Ouchi published his book *Theory Z*, but not much improvement seems to have been made in corporate America. The level of trust in those well-performing firms may have improved. To what extent the way American managers and workers communicate has become more subtle, using fewer linguistic codes, seems difficult to judge. The topic of intimacy has definitely become a most controversial one in American organizations, one much complicated by such touchy issues as sexual harassment.

Among the three golden values, subtlety is the most relevant to our discussion of rules and regulations. Relationships between people are always complex, and work process (such as teamwork) is always changing. A manager who knows his or her people well can tell each person's personalities, strong points versus weak points, and put together work teams of maximum effectiveness. "These subtleties can never be captured explicitly, and any bureaucratic rule will do violence to them" (Ouchi 1981, p. 6).

To melt rules and regulations into team culture and increase the level of subtlety, an organization or team should encourage the use of high-contexting communication, which occurs in the thickness of human relationships. High-contexting communication is one in which the mass of information or meaning is not in the explicit linguistic codes (rules and regulations in this context) but in the context of communication, in the reading of nonverbal messages, in the subtlety of human relationships (Hall 1991). According to Hall, contexting, which is a screening process by which humans determine what they pay attention to and what they do not attend to, involves two different but interrelated processes—one inside the organism and the other outside. "The first takes place in the brain and is a function of either past experience (programmed, internalized contexting) or the structure of the nervous system (innate contexting), or both. External contexting comprises the situation and/or setting in which an event occurs (situational and/or environmental contexting)" (pp. 50–51). For example, two team members who have been working together for an extended period of time could understand each other perfectly without even saying a word; their shared experiences (or team culture) have programmed them in such a way that they will be able to cooperate without resorting to any linguistic codes or bureaucratic rules.

It seems that team culture, which is built upon such values as trust, subtlety, and intimacy and which has incorporated rules and regulations, can handle organizational complexities much more efficiently than the linguistic codes written on the paper or posted on the wall. This is because team culture permits one to exercise self-control, which can be practiced any time, any way to respond to competitive market needs.

INJECTING FLUIDITY INTO ROLE DEFINITIONS

An organizational role, in the traditional sense, is a set of expected recurring behavioral patterns that an organization member engages in within a functional boundary and at a certain hierarchical level. One is not supposed to cross his/her functional boundary to do what he/she is not assigned to do. Deviations from role definitions are perceived to be threatening to an orderly organizational life and, therefore, may be severely punished.

Rigid role definitions, often closely associated with an over-layered hierarchy and excessive rules and regulations, render organization members unable to deal with the unexpected and thus reduce an organization's responsiveness to market needs. The potential harm of enforcing rigid role definitions, which threatens even a traditional organization, can be kept at its minimum level if the tasks that workers are assigned to perform are of a routine nature and the market the organization deals with is stable. In a high-speed environment where anything is possible any time, rigid role definitions, like straitjackets, prevent organization members from moving quickly and taking whatever actions necessary to cope with the changes that occurred just last night. The consequence involved isn't difficult to imagine.

With an organization's over-layered hierarchy flattened and its rules and regulations simplified, the next thing to do is to inject fluidity into role definitions. *Fluid role definitions indeed are another basic requirement of effective teamwork in an organization that follows high-speed management premises.* In order for a team member to perform a multifunction/multiresponsibility role, an organization that follows high-speed management philosophy must see to it that the team member master a variety of skills. The following list of skills represents what a team member may be expected to acquire:

Job skills:
- equipment operation
- process control
- safe work practices
- interpretation and application of company information
- maintenance skills

Team and interaction skills:
- orientation to teams and teamwork
- team design concepts
- listening and giving feedback
- one-to-one communication
- techniques for handling conflict and reaching consensus
- valuing diversity
- training and coaching others
- presentation skills
- meeting skills

- meeting facilitation
- selection of team members
- assessment of the team's performance

Quality and problem-solving skills:
- clarification of the customers' requirements
- identification of quality involvement opportunities
- quality tools and techniques
- development and selection of solutions
- quality improvement planning
- ongoing quality assurance
- statistical process control

(Wellins and George 1991, p. 30)

This is by no means a complete list, but it is already a lot, much more than what an average worker would normally be required to master to perform his or her clearly defined job. Multi-skilling can be achieved through job rotation or team training programs, and it can be reinforced by a pay-for-skills reward system.

The role of a leader of a team-based organization should be changed from planner/controller to coach/facilitator. Instead of telling team members what to do, his or her job is now to teach them how to lead themselves. Skills training is a must not only for average team members but also for leaders, who also should be trained in the skills unique to their roles—such as coaching for success, encouraging initiative, leading successful meetings, and reinforcing effective performance (Wellins and George 1991).

For many team-based organizations, the line between the role of a leader and that of an average worker seems to have become very fuzzy. It is becoming increasingly difficult for an outsider to tell leaders from those who are led. Their roles have become very much overlapped. In some other organizations, leaders, midlevel leaders in particular, are fast vanishing. Their roles are being assumed by team members themselves (it is likely that a former leader has simply become a team member). It is possible to have not only a "bossless team" but a "bossless organization." However, the possibility of a bossless team or bossless organization does not mean that leadership is no longer needed for a team-based organization following high-speed management premises. It means that leadership is "distributed" among individual team members (Barry 1991). It means that leadership is now exerted more from within each and every team member than from outside by somebody who is called "leader." It also means that leadership has been melted into the role of an average team member.

What kind of structure will emerge when an organization's over-layered hierarchy is flattened, its many rules and regulations simplified, and its members' roles expanded? To what extent can this kind of structure increase its adaptability and responsiveness to the environment? And how representative is it of the high-speed management philosophy? To answer these questions is our next task.

ADAPTIVE ORGANIZATION

An adaptive organization is one that is formed by the task, not by a pre-designed structure. It is one, as an MIT sociologist, Charles Sabel, suggests, that has no identifiable top or bottom, beginning or end, and constantly turns in on itself, in an endless cycle of creation and destruction (Dumaine 1991). *It is one that is defined more by external environmental variables than by internal management logics. In a word, it is one that constantly adapts to keep its competitive advantage.* This is still more an ideal than a reality, but aspects of it are taking shape. Dumaine writes that the organization of the future will still retain some vestiges of the old hierarchy. Spinning around the straight lines will be a vertiginous pattern of constantly changing teams, task forces, partnerships, and other informal structures. It will be like a group of dancers forming a flower on stage, disbanding into chaos, and then regrouping to form a flag or something else. Like the dancers, in tomorrow's corporation teams variously composed of shop-floor workers, managers, technical experts, suppliers, and customers will join together to do a job and then disband, with everyone going off to the next assignment (Dumaine 1991).

It seems clear that an adaptive organization is one that, instead of organizing its work along traditional structural lines, is based on teams whose formation is determined by what the tasks are at the time of formation. The degree of its adaptiveness depends very much on the degree of stability or instability of the environment. There is a continuum from a formal organization to an adaptive one (fig. 5.4).

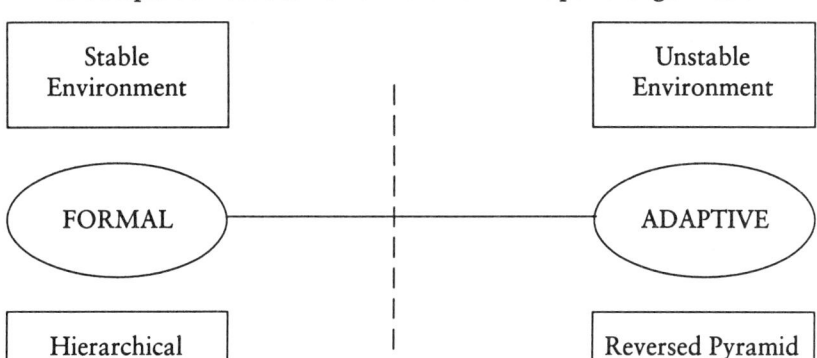

FIGURE 53
A Comparison between a Formal and an Adaptive Organization

Stable Environment		Unstable Environment
FORMAL	————————	ADAPTIVE
Hierarchical Functional		Reversed Pyramid Cross-Functional

As shown in the continuum, formal organizations characterized by a vertical hierarchy and horizontal divisions of functions fit with a stable environment that is very much predictable. *As the degree of instability of environment gets higher, the organization moves gradually from the formal end to the adaptive end, flattening its hierarchy and removing barriers that block cross-functional cooperation.* In a formal organization, the way the task gets completed is defined by the hierarchy and division of functional responsibilities. In an adaptive organization, the nature of the task defines the organizational structure, which is more processual than static, in the sense that various teams are formed, disbanded, reformed, and disbanded again. It is not an overexaggeration to claim that *an adaptive organization should be team based.*

It is team based because this is how employees become empowered. In a team-based adaptive organization, employees, instead of waiting to be told what to do, decide what they know or believe is the best for the work and the organization as a whole. This is called "decentralization," and it provides openings for innovation and creativity and greatly unleashes employee energy that would have been suppressed in a hierarchical organization. When the employees really have the freedom to make decisions on the assembly line or in an emergency situation, the principle of high-speed management can truly be carried out.

One of the most interesting paradoxes facing an adaptive organization is that while decentralization, which empowers teams and employees, is definitely the trend, there is at the same time increasing centralization of information and control, which has been made possible by the availability of sophisticated information and communication technologies. For example, Cypress, a specialty computer chips company, has developed a computer system that is capable of tracking all its fifteen hundred employees as they are scattered in different functions, teams, and projects. Apple is developing a computer called Spider that can instantly tell a manager whether an employee is available to join his or her project, what the employee's skills are, and where he or she is located in the corporation. The Spider system combines a network of personal computers with a video-conferencing system and a database of employee records. A manager forming a team can call up profiles of employees regardless of where they are. On the screen he or she will see a color photo of the person, where he works, who reports to him/her, whom he/she reports to, and his/her skills (Dumaine 1991).

The processes of decentralization and centralization going hand in hand generate a structure that is extremely flexible and yet highly controlled. This structure characterizes what is here called the "adaptive organization." Adaptive organizations, besides using their internal flexibility and increasing use of teams, tend to take an interest in alliances, partnerships, joint ventures, and other relationships with parties from outside. This leads us to another new organizational structure called "virtual organization." Whereas some organizational writers may decline to make a clear distinction between adaptive organization and virtual organization, we use the latter to refer mainly to a firm's alliance or network with parties outside its structural boundary. In the next few lines, we will see how important teamwork is to a virtual organization.

VIRTUAL ORGANIZATION

Virtual organization is "a temporary network of independent companies—suppliers, customers, even erstwhile rivals—linked by information technology to share skills, costs, and access to one another's markets. It will have neither central office nor organization chart. It will have no hierarchy, no vertical integration" ("Virtual Organization" 1993, p. 99). The inception of the concept of the virtual organization is indeed a high-speed management response to information and communication technological revolutions, markets' unpredictability, and a single company's inability to do everything better than others. As James R. Houghton, chairman of Corning Inc., points out, "Technologies are changing so fast that nobody can do it all alone anymore" ("Virtual Organization" 1993, p. 100). Corning enjoys the best reputation of managing alliances, that is, the virtual organization. Other companies that have been exploring the benefit of using the concept include AT&T, MCI, Apple Computer, Motorola, and IBM.

These companies' interest in the concept of the virtual organization comes from one single belief: a business entity that is composed of the best of everything has the potential to have competitive advantage. So ideally, or theoretically, a virtual organization is one that is composed of companies that all contribute their very best and all benefit from the network. *It is a collection of all the "core competencies" contributed by participating partners.*

Although there have been success stories such as the one about Corning, all the benefits the virtual organization claims seem to be more theoretical than real, at least for the time being. The key to success seems to lie in whether or not participating companies are willing to share resources, including critical information regarding each other's "core competencies," and whether or not teamwork is likely to follow after the formation of the alliance. Like benefits, risks are always there. For example, what may happen if you lose control of the function that you cede to your partners? What would you do if proprietary information or technology have "legally" escaped? Structurally, the challenges could be even larger. How could you build mutual trust with outsiders or with people you would work with for no more than, for instance, six months?

Teamwork is probably the best guarantee for the success of a virtual organization, which typically has no vertical integration, no formal leaders, no strictly defined rules and regulations, and above all, no traditions to follow. Instead, "teams of people in different companies would routinely work together, concurrently rather than sequentially, via computer network in real time. Artificial-intelligence systems and sensing devices would connect engineers directly to the production line" ("Virtual Organization" 1993, pp. 100–101). Structurally speaking, a virtual organization is teams based. It is not a network of participating companies. Rather, it is a network of teams from various participating companies. In the final analysis, the virtual organization depends upon interorganizational teamwork for its success. Teamwork is the key to success simply because the almost-no-structure virtual organization so demands.

CHAPTER 6

Team Anchorage in Organizational Life

As has been discussed in the previous chapters, teams and teamwork are a central focus of inquiry in high-speed management. The emergence of high-performance teams, including self-managed teams, cross-functional teams, and executive level teams with fluid and flexible structures, has come as a direct response to an increasingly uncertain and volatile business environment and, as a result, the revolutionization of organizational management philosophies and practices. One of the easiest things for a manager to know to manage a traditionally structured organization is that you don't have to bother to figure out who does what, where and when, and reports to whom. All departments and sections, and presumably all organization members, know where to "position" themselves in terms of the tasks each is set to perform, the amount of power one is allowed to wield, and the rules and regulations you are required to follow. Organizational positioning, or anchorage, is not a big problem. You don't have to position or anchor yourself; you are positioned or anchored by the organization.

Coupled with mounting corporate interest in the dynamism of intraorganizational teamwork is a recent trend in the rise of an increasing number of the so-called "modular corporations" whose competitive advantage very much depends upon interorganizational teamwork. Dell Computer and Chrysler, for example, using smooth teamwork with their suppliers, are stealing customers from rigid, vertically integrated rivals like IBM and General Motors (Tully 1993). Typically, a modular company focuses on a core competency and outsources the rest, and the engine of their worldwide competitiveness is well managed interorganizational teamwork. From a team anchorage perspective, the company and its suppliers may well be conceptualized as a collection

---

Portions of this chapter were published in M. Cross and W. Cummins, eds., *The Proceedings of the Fifth Conference on Corporate Communication,* Fairleigh Dickinson University, Madison, N.J., 1993.

of teams whose collaboration with one another composes what is here called "interorganizational teamwork." Implied in this conceptualization is the notion of how a company, be it a modular type or a nonmodular type, should position or anchor itself in the interorganizational field (Kreps 1990).

In a high-speed age in which everybody wants to cut your throat, things are not that simple for organizations, various departments and sections in an organization, and individual organization members. *It is now probably the case that you are forced to constantly anchor and reanchor yourself in order to survive and prosper as much as you are, in a traditionally structural sense, anchored by the organization.* How an organization, viewed as a team in the interorganizational field, is anchored or anchors itself in the larger volatile business environment is becoming increasingly complex. Organizational anchorage, both intra and inter, has become very much a processual problem as well as a structural problem.

Instead of discussing in detail organizational anchorage in a general way, we will, in this chapter, go inside an organization or an interorganizational field to examine how teams and individual team members should anchor themselves in organizational life. To accomplish such a task, we will first briefly review the basic premises of high-speed management and their relevancy to team anchorage in organizational life. We will then identify and analyze four dimensions of team anchorage in a high-speed management environment. These are task or structural anchorage, symbolic or cultural anchorage, human needs or psychological anchorage, and member skills anchorage in both intra- and interorganizational contexts. This is followed by a brief discussion of the nature of team anchorage in a high-speed business environment. The importance of a careful manipulation of the relativity of structural stability versus processual change will be the focus of such a discussion.

PREMISES OF HIGH-SPEED MANAGEMENT AND THEIR RELEVANCY TO TEAM ANCHORAGE IN ORGANIZATIONAL LIFE

High-speed management is used by organizations with a view to sustaining their competitive advantage in an increasingly uncertain and volatile environment. This environment is characterized by rapidly changing technology, quick market saturation, and unexpected global competition, which makes succeeding in business, international business in particular, very difficult (Cushman and King 1992; Fraker 1984). This environment has led to the emergence of high-speed management for coping with a volatile business climate. The key features implied in the high-speed management premises are best knowledge of your customers' needs as well as your competitors' newest moves, new products development, close coordination among functional units, quality of products; an adaptive and flexible culture, and global scanning. These key points combine to suggest that there are four mutually inclusive components of high-speed management:

1. speed-to-market with quality products or services as a chief goal
2. environmental scanning as a basic tool
3. an organization's value chain—internal and external, horizontal and vertical—as a fundamental guarantee of corporate competitiveness
4. integration, coordination, and control as three main management and communication processes at both the intraorganizational and interorganizational levels

Here in this chapter we take a special interest in the relevancy of these high-speed management principles to the notion of team anchorage. As has been indicated at the beginning of this chapter, team anchorage refers to how a team is positioned and positions itself in the organization or the larger interorganizational field in terms of task performance, cultural bonding, resources sharing, and individual members' skills development. Such positioning, from a high-speed management perspective, is very much determined by how a team should facilitate the achieving of the goal of speed-to-market with new quality products or services, how it uses data and/or data analyses acquired from environmental scanning to inform itself of the dynamics of the market, how it understands the nature of synergistic process involved in the organizational value chain, and how it contributes to as well as benefits from organizational integration, coordination, and control at various levels. Let's explain.

As far as speed-to-market with new quality products or services is concerned, no team can function effectively or even has a reason to exist if it fails to accept the concept of time or speed as offering a main competitive advantage across all markets and product lines. The desperate drive for speed-to-market is the direct result of shrinking product life cycles and a corporation's quest for higher profits. A McKinsey & Co. study reported that a product six months late to market misses out as much as one-third of the potential profit over the product's lifetime (Vessey 1991). Quantum, a fast-growing marketer of disk drives based in California, has had a partnership with Japan's Matsushita-Kotobuki Electronics (MKE) for eight years. Desperately driven by speed-to-market, at each stage in designing a new market, Quantum's engineers send the newest drawings to a production team at MKE. And MKE constantly propose changes in design that make new disk drives easier to manufacture. When the product is ready for production, eight to ten Quantum engineers would descend on MKE's plant in western Japan for at least a month. To facilitate smooth teamwork, Quantum is offering courses in Japanese language and culture. The close collaboration pays off. Quantum introduced in 1992 the ProDrive ELS, a new disk drive for desktops that quickly became a favorite with such PC sellers as Dell and AST Research. With speed-to-market in mind and by teaming with MKE, Quantum, dubbed a "modular corporation," was able to design the product in fourteen months, about half the industry average (Tully 1993).

To do environmental scanning, a corporation must possess a fast and accurate intelligence system that is capable of obtaining, firstly, information regarding the economic, political, and cultural trends in the larger environment and, secondly, information regarding industry-market dynamics. The first scanning activity, extensive information search, scans a few dimensions of a large number of heterogeneous societal trends. The second type, intensive information search, scans a large number of dimensions in homogeneous industries-markets (Kovavic 1992; Geertz 1978). Environmental scanning is an "enacting" process in which the team of scanners not only gather information from the environment but assign meanings to the information gathered. This is a most challenging task. One person alone can't possibly assume the task; it requires a team consisting of top management, professionals with highly sophisticated technical expertise, and a bunch of well qualified strategists. It is not only that effective environmental scanning requires teamwork; environmental scanning is also a precondition for the functioning of teams at both intraorganizational and interorganizational levels. For example, an organization lacking information about the dynamics of its unique industry-market and the dynamics of the larger societal environment will not be able to strategically position itself as a team member in the interorganizational field.

Value chain theory (Rockart and Short 1989; Cushman and King 1992) is a third main component of high-speed management. Value chain, simply defined, is a series of discrete activities and processes involved in producing a product or service. Functional unit activities and business processes may either add value to or reduce the value of a product or service; this has direct bearing on a firm's competitive advantage. The value chain of a firm typically starts from its suppliers, goes through such functional units as design, engineering, purchasing, manufacturing, distribution, sales, and service, and ends at customers. Since both the suppliers and customers exist outside the boundary of the firm, the value chain is never a closed system. Both intraorganizational and interorganizational dimensions of the chain need to be carefully and constantly examined by high-speed managers. Cutting through various functional unit activities are three business processes, namely, product development, product delivery, and customer service. Each process includes some activities unique to itself and some activities overlapping with other business processes. It is important to point out that the design of a value chain can be both horizontal and vertical. The linkages between various functional units seem to be horizontal. As far as each functional unit is concerned, it may well be conceived as a sub value chain that may include, for example, the primary line people and support staff.

As almost implied in the word *chain,* the mechanism of the value chain of any organization is smooth teamwork that maintains linkages among all functional unit activities and business processes. In other words, talking about value chain is talking about teamwork at almost all levels. Team anchorage is one of the most crucial issues that need to be addressed seriously, because it has become much more complicated in the present high-speed age than in previous times. Team anchorage in the value chain of an organization is multidimensional, involving such levels as task performance, human needs congruence, cultural fit, and skills requirement. Adding to the complexity is the paradox of stability versus flexibility inherent in team anchorage in organizations that need to respond constantly and speedily to the highly uncertain and volatile business environment.

The fourth component of high-speed management comprises the three management and communication processes of integration, coordination, and control (Cushman and King 1992). Integration is the use of communication to achieve "oneness" in goals to strive for and values to uphold. Coordination is the process in which team members share information and reach behavioral congruence critical to the production of a product or service. Control is the use of sophisticated information and communication systems to audit production and management processes and then come up with ways of correcting deviations from the preset goals. Integration, coordination, and control are, indeed, the very process of teamwork, which, by nature, is a communication process. As indicated at the beginning of the chapter, team anchorage is not only a structural entity but also a process that involves change. Integration, coordination, and control are the processes through which teams and team members constantly examine their positioning in the organization and the larger environment.

Having discussed briefly the relevancy of the four basic premises of high-speed management to team anchorage in organizational life, we can now take a look at some of the more important dimensions of team anchorage from a high-speed management perspective.

DIMENSIONS OF TEAM ANCHORAGE

We will discuss four dimensions of team anchorage: structural anchorage, cultural anchorage, psychological anchorage, and skills anchorage.

Structural Anchorage

Structural Anchorage pertains to task performance. Classical approach to organizational structure is based on strict adherence to hierarchical order, rules and regulations, division of labor, span of control, upward reporting relationships, and so on. External environmental pressure, increasing internal organizational complexity, and intensified competition in the global as well as national/regional economies and the desperate speed-to-market drive have demanded that organizational structure be leaner with fewer layers of management, more employee involvement and participation, and more flexibility in classical variables such as rules and regulations. The popularity of team concept is, indeed, the very result of the influence of these environmental changes on organizations. Teams, whether they are project-based, self-managing, or cross-functional, defy artificial barriers between functional units and encourage worker involvement and participation in the management as well as production processes. Team environment is more, or much more, challenging to individual team members, since they are now required to take initiatives to position themselves, instead of being passively positioned, in the organizational structure in an efficient and responsible way.

Teams differ fundamentally from formal groups in the classical sense in the way that organizational life is structured. There are three patterns that formal groups follow (Lefton and Buzzotta 1988). The first, the hierarchical pattern, emphasizes rank. For task completion, hierarchical groups have strict procedures for downward transmission and downward control. Under the hierarchical pattern, both the group and the individual group members are positioned or rigidly anchored in the task structure to do what they are told to do, leaving little room for deviation or flexibility. The second is the formalistic pattern, which emphasizes impersonal organization and bureaucratic transactions. When this pattern is followed, nothing is larger than preset rules and regulations. Innovation and boundary crossing are never encouraged; one is nailed to one's position, which is defined by nothing but a set of rigid bureaucratic rules. The third pattern, the circular, goes to the other extreme by being totally structureless; individual group members have the luxury of choosing to do whatever they please. The number one principle of the circular approach is to make sure that everyone gets along well with everyone else. Whereas the first two patterns pertain to rigid structural and formalistic anchorage in organizational life, this third one has no anchorage at all, letting the boat float in whatever direction is dictated by the wind or current.

As opposed to the three possible work patterns of a classically designed formal group, the teamwork pattern encourages the enlisting of the entire group, including all group members in such activities as goal setting, planning, problem solving, and decision making (Lefton and Buzzotta, 1988). The team and team members not only are actively involved in the production process but also may take over managerial duties such as work and vacation scheduling, ordering materials, and even hiring new members (Hoerr 1989). Under the teamwork pattern, necessary structure is still respected, necessary rules and regulations are still followed, but team members and the team as a whole are encouraged to participate fully in team processes and the larger organizational life in order to deal with an increasingly competitive business environment.

Reporting relationships become much less rigid and more fluid under the teamwork pattern. Such teams as project teams, problem-solving teams, and innovation teams may have a relatively short life span. When the task is completed, the team is dissolved. Yet within its short life span, reporting relationships can be complicated. A common problem is to whom an individual team member should report his/her work, the team leader (if there is one), or the head of the functional unit where s/he came from? This is exactly an "anchorage" problem. To take a more fluid approach would be to position oneself in the team that one is assigned to and report to the team leader, but behave in such a way which would suggest that one still cares about one's original functional unit and respects its leader. To state this more clearly, a team member should anchor himself or herself relatively solidly in the team in terms of task performance, yet not forget that one foot is still in his or her former functional unit to which he or she may have a high chance of returning.

Task-structural anchorage is also relevant to a whole organization when it is viewed as a team in the interorganizational field. As Tully (1993) reported, in a leap of industrial evolution as a response to changes in a high-speed business environment, many companies are shunning vertical integration for a lean, nimble structure centered on what they do best. The new breed avoid becoming monoliths laden with plants and bureaucracy. Instead, they are changing themselves into hubs surrounded by networks of the world's best suppliers. Modular firms, which are flourishing in apparel and electronics industries that sell trendy products at high speed, tend to anchor themselves in a "core competency," focusing on such tasks as market research, new product development, hiring the best engineers, and training sales or service personnel. They outsource all the rest which other companies do better and cheaper. It seems crucial to the survival and prosperity of a firm that it understand the importance of the strategic anchorage and do it well.

Cultural Anchorage

Cultural anchorage is probably the most paradoxical of the four dimensions that we are discussing in this chapter, in that culture by nature is conservative and therefore genetically resists change, but high-speed management emphasizes innovativeness, responsiveness, and flexibility, all of which involve the very notion of change. Where should a team and team members position or anchor themselves in the organizational life in terms of shared values and behavioral patterns? Or is there any culture to talk about when everything is so fluid and uncertain in a high-speed environment? Is it possible to institutionalize the idea of "fluid anchorage?"

Here we are talking about both cultural stability and flexibility as required by the high-speed management philosophy. Indeed cultural stability, or a shared and cohesive culture, instead of being a clear structure, is an invisible force that gives a team its drive (Bolman and Deal, 1991). But flexibility, in terms of structure or operations or role descriptions or cultural interpretations of organizational life, is a core concept in high-speed management. To solve this paradox, we need to create two conceptual tools, namely, *higher-order values* (HOVs) *and lower-order values* (LOVs). HOVs are defined as cultural values that relate to more general organizational goals and management principles and should stay relatively stable, even in a highly turbulent and chaotic environment. In contrast, LOVs are cultural values that relate to more specific organizational tasks and management strategies and techniques and should be made flexible enough to be able to adapt to environmental changes.

We feel that this HOVs vs LOVs distinction is conceptually relevant and practically useful, as we have been constantly warned by organizational researchers of a chaotic and turbulent environment that seems to be rendering doing business so vulnerable that there is nothing people can feel certain about. Tom Peters warned five years ago: "No company is safe . . . [f]or the foreseeable future, there is no such thing as a 'solid,' or even substantial, lead over one's competitors.... Excellent firms of tomorrow will cherish impermanence—and thrive on chaos" (Peters 1987, pp. 34). To support Peters's argument, we suggest that the concept of LOVs implies the same notion of "impermanence," that is, being ready to change when and where necessary. However, a misreading of the statements like the above may lead to a belief that nothing really is or should be stable in today's organizations, and business organizations in particular, which is quite untrue.

As has been borne out by numerous success stories, stable cultural anchorage, either at the team level or the level of individual team members, is a main success factor. One of the more perceptive articles on corporate culture is John Nicholls's "An Alloplastic Approach to Corporate Culture." Nicholls writes:

> Much of what is written in the 'business press' is like feeding horror stories to someone who is already living in a nightmare: it confirms his fears and strengthen his resolve to change but offers little practical help in the way of signposts or guidelines.... Even worse is the implication that all experience is becoming invalid. The world has become topsy-turvy, it is suggested, that the state in which Macbeth reached in his madness in which 'nothing is but what is not' has now been achieved by most of humanity.... It is evident, however, that even in the most turbulent of environments, some things remain unchanged. New conditions never completely invalidate all of one's experience. (Nicholls 1985, p. 36)

We argue that even when change is completely turbulent and chaotic, an organization's HOVs should stay relatively stable. Teams and individual team members should anchor themselves relatively solidly in such HOVs as respect for the individual, service to the customer, superior accomplishment of all tasks, effective management, obligations to stockholders," and "fair deal for the supplier." It should not be surprising that one sees striking similarities in HOVs held by different organizations in vastly different industries.

As opposed to HOVs, LOVs are a set of corporate values that relate to more specific organizational tasks and management strategies and practices (such as sales, investment, and marketing), and therefore they are subject to change due to environmental changes. This nature of LOVs implies a constant contradiction between stability and flexibility, a contradiction that, if not managed well, may create serious confusion for an organization. So here we introduce the idea of fluid anchorage, a kind of anchorage that permits vertical or lateral movement of what is anchored. Fluid cultural anchorage is a short-term anchorage: a team or team member may quickly disengage itself or himself from an experience, no matter how rewarding it once was, so that new action may be taken to respond to environmental contingencies.

A superior performing team should solidly and flexibly anchor itself in a corporate culture that is a mixture of a solid and stable HOV system and a flexible and adaptable LOV system. A differentiation between the two value categories is necessary and useful, but too sharp a distinction is not only impossible but also harmful. Indeed there is no clear-cut demarcation line between the two; the line is always fluid. A higher-order value, under certain circumstances, may gradually become a lower-order one, and vice versa. Some values may well be called "in-betweens" in the hierarchy, their going up or down being determined by many a contingency.

Psychological Anchorage

By *psychological anchorage*, we try to address the issue of what may be called "human needs compatibility" between an organization and its individual team members. Individual team members' needs may or may not always coincide with organizational needs including, for example, the need of the organization meeting its goals. Any mutually satisfying solution to any of the potential conflicts depends on mutual understanding and collaboration between individual members and the organization. This means that both sides should understand that the high level of global competitiveness, galloping technological change, and customer and client demands for increased responsiveness have made flexibility in production processes and rapid product throughput highly desirable (Kolodny and Dresner 1986). This also means that neither side should neglect the needs of the other in order to come up with this "flexibility in production processes and rapid product throughput." Individual team members should know how to position themselves in such a way that facilitates reaching a fit between the two sets of needs. The organization, on the other hand, should acknowledge such "psychological positioning" or "psychological anchorage" as being legitimate and as equally important as "structural anchorage" and "cultural anchorage." As a matter of fact, many organizations have now come to the understanding that "programmable equipment and an adaptable work force are two crucial elements in any response to the demands for flexibility." And standardized roles with fixed descriptions and expectations are not the ingredients of adaptability (Kolodny and Dresner 1986, p. 35). Organizations should be sure to grant individuals and the teams they belong to the autonomy in work-related decision making and to recognize their need for self-actualization, security, respect, and self-growth.

America possesses soil in which individualistic ideas grow easily. This discussion on individual autonomy in organizational life never fails to appeal even to those performance- and profit-conscious, classically oriented managers. Placing too much emphasis on individual needs satisfaction without talking about the fate of the organization, however, is always risky. When the whole ship sinks, all individual sailors die. *In a fast-changing, highly uncertain business environment like the one we are now living in, the fate of any size organization is subject to the mandate of an increasingly unfriendly environment. Having this unique feature in mind, individual organization members, whether they are performing in a team or in their traditional functional unit, should realistically position or anchor themselves in "negotiating" with the organization over needs or interests issues.*

The joint optimization of individual needs satisfaction and organizational goals definition tends to put teams at their peak performance. No teams can function in their best possible ways for any extended period of time if individual team members' needs are not attended to. And no teams even have a reason to exist if the larger organization lacks the support of individual members and cannot survive by reaching its basic goals.

Skills Anchorage

Although work teams differ from company to company, they typically consist of five to twelve multiskilled workers who rotate jobs and produce an entire product or service with only minimal supervision (Hoerr 1989). Team-based organizations pay more attention to employee skills training. Such training can be broken into several categories such as job skills (Wellins and George 1991), which include all the technical knowledge and skills that team members need to perform on the job. Team members are often expected to learn all the jobs on the team through a job rotation or multiskilling system.

Team members may also be expected to master some leadership skills and knowledge that are typically reserved for managers and supervisors. This could be threatening to midlevel managers and supervisors whose jobs may be eliminated. Barry (1991) has identified four clusters of leadership roles and skills for members of self-managing teams: envisioning skills, organizing skills, spanning skills, and social skills. Envisioning skills include facilitating idea generation and innovation, defining and championing overall goals, finding conceptual links between systems, and fostering frame-breaking thinking. Organizing skills pertain to the knowledge of managing details, deadlines, time, efficiency, and structure. Spanning skills involve facilitating activities needed to link with outside groups and individuals. Social skills focus on maintaining a harmonious work relationship among team members.

Not all team members are required to master these skills, but it will definitely put a member in a difficult situation if one does not have any, since such skills could be crucial for high performance in a high-speed management environment. Teams and team members will have their positions challenged if they are found to be poorly trained in these various skills. To have a relatively secure position and perform to the requirement of high-speed management, teams and team members must know when and where to anchor themselves in these skill areas.

Having discussed the four types of team anchorage, we are in a position to take a closer look at the nature of team anchorage in organizational life from a high-speed management perspective.

STABILITY AND FLEXIBILITY: THE DYNAMIC NATURE OF TEAM ANCHORAGE IN A HIGH-SPEED AGE

Paradoxically, stability and flexibility are the dual nature of team anchorage in a high-speed age. A high-speed management organization is like a high-speed moving car on a superhighway; when you are driving, you and your passengers (who are teams or individual team members) must sit solidly and stabley, all with seatbelts securely fastened, so that you can drive safely. Yet, if anything unexpected happens on the superhighway, you and your passengers must be able to get out of your seats to handle the situation; you must be movable and flexible.

Stability pertains to structure. It is always possible, albeit difficult at times, to pinpoint the structure or structures of a team's anchorage at the task, cultural, psychological, and skills levels, that is, to tell what it "looks like" at an artificially "frozen" moment. But this is never a static structure; rather, it is what we may call an "informal structure," or a "flexible structure." You must build into this structure enough "flexibility" or "fluidity" so that your team can swiftly change its position to respond to fast-changing environmental challenges.

In a highly chaotic business environment, team anchorage in organizational life must, first of all, be rock solid: you must be able to clearly define your task or tasks for a certain period of time; you must have certain values and believe in something; you must be able to identify team member needs, on the one hand, and organizational needs, on the other; and you must know what skills are required of each team member and the team as a whole. And this is what we mean by stability or structure. As we have noted, your seat-belt must be securely fastened before you can drive at high speed and safely.

But *high-speed management deals with high-speed change.* Indeed, the very notion of team or teamwork, which deviates from a rigid hierarchy, is associated with worker participation, flexibility, and change. One of the primary tasks facing each and every team of a high-speed management organization is how to manage change—*change in the environment, change in the organization, and change in its positioning or anchorage in the organization and the larger environment.* Such change can be incremental or fundamental or even as radical as "self-destruction"—disbanding the organization—in order to come up with new strategic alliances, either intraorganizationally or interorganizationally.

Managing the balance between stability and flexibility is always easier said than done in a high-speed age. Going to either extreme at any critical moment could bring unwanted results to the team and the organization—and sometimes unsalvageable disasters. For a team to perform to the satisfaction of high-speed management, it must know very well where it stands today and where to go tomorrow.

CHAPTER 7

A Negotiated Linking Program: Communication Strategies for Coaligning an Organization's Internal and External Resources with Its Competitive Environment

> Successful organizations achieve strategic fit with their market environment and support their strategies with appropriately designed structures and management processes, less successful organizations typically exhibit poor fit externally and/or internally. (Miles and Snow 1984, p. 10)

A rationale is provided for these claims based upon four distinctions that characterize an organization's capacity to negotiate an appropriate coalignment or linking strategy with its customers and then orders its organizational structures and processes in a manner appropriate to operationalizing its strategic fit.

> *Minimal fit* among strategy, structure, and process is essential to all organizations operating in competitive environments. If a misfit occurs for a prolonged period, the result usually is failure.
>
> *Tight fit*, both internally and externally, is associated with excellence. Tight fit is the underlying causal synamic producing sustained, excellent performance and a strong corporate culture.
>
> *Early fit*, the discovery and articulation of a new pattern of strategy, structures, and process, frequently results in performance records which in sporting circles would merit Hall of Fame status. The invention or early application of a new organization form may provide a more powerful competitive advantage than a market or technological breakthrough.
>
> *Fragile fit* involves vulnerability to both shifting external conditions and to inadvertent internal unraveling. Even Hall of Fame organization may become victims of deteriorating fit. (10–11)

Successful organizational coalignment or fit is both a state and a process. In practical terms, the basic alignment mechanism is some communication strategy for coaligning the various parts of an organization's value chain in such a manner as to take advantage of one's competitors' weaknesses while forming a tight fit with one's customers. However, since competitors tend to learn quickly from their mistakes and adjust, organizational coalignment activities constitute an ongoing process of continuously improving an organization's fit with its environment so as to sustain its competitive advantage.

Until now, little attention has been paid to explicating communication strategies for coaligning an organization's internal and external resources with its competitive environment. It will be the purpose of this chapter to explicate and illustrate such a strategic theory. To achieve this purpose, we will revisit two key components of high-speed management—environmental scanning and value chain theory—and the role they play in an organization's coalignment process. But first we need to conceptualize coalignment and understand its nature.

THE NATURE AND FUNCTIONS OF COALIGNMENT

Coalignment is a unique form of organizational interdependence in which each of the units or elements in a firm's value chain clearly articulates their needs, concerns, and potential contributions to an organization's functioning in such a manner that management can utilize this information to forge an appropriate value-added configuration and sustainable competitive advantage to the linkages. An appropriate value-added pattern of linkages among units is one in which management can integrate, coordinate and control each unit's needs, concerns, and contributions so that the outcome is mutually satisfying to the units involved and optimizing in value-added activities of the organization as a whole. Coalignment viewed as such constitutes internal and external organizational teamwork.

World-class benchmarking, which we discussed in chapter 3, sets the standards or targets for improving organizational performance. These benchmarks or goals to be met in improving an organization's ability to respond to environmental change must be set at a world-class level if one is to establish a competitive advantage. Only then will improvements in an organization's external and internal linkages or coalignment process provide the value-added gains necessary for sustainable competitive advantage.

The value chain (for a review of value chain theory, see chapter 2) as the organizational structure and processes requires coalignment or teamwork. From a management perspective, the particular configuration of an organization's value chain and its linkages creates several very specific problems.

First, it is important to understand that in different types of markets (i.e., mature, export, service, declining, etc.), the continuous improvement of some functional unit and/or business processes are more important to maintaining or gaining market shares, while others are less important or not important at all (Venkatraman and Prescott 1990).

Second, it may be the case that due to certain external linking activities such as joint ventures, technical alliances or outsourcing, and so forth, that certain parts of the value chain will reside partially or wholly within other organizations. However, the value-added activity of that other organization's contribution to our firm's value chain can be realized only when the two organizations are appropriately coaligned. Thus, the effective use of continuous-improvement programs to coalign these value-added activities resides in the other firm or between the two firms. If many such linkages exist or only a few exist but are critical to the product's performance, then control of the value chain will reside outside the firm. In all cases, appropriate monitoring and control processes must be established (Kanter 1989).

Third, the functional units and/or business processes of a firm's value chain may be located anywhere on the globe where value-added activity or competitive advantage may be gained yet continuous-improvement programs must transcend these geographic distances.

Product development processes of the value chain are normally located in regions where firms have access to a steady supply of state-of-the-art engineers such as in Japan, the United States and Germany where competitive advantage can be obtained from product differentiation. Product delivery processes are normally located near sources of inexpensive skilled labor as it is a case of production facilities in Mexico, Spain, China, and Singapore where competitive advantage comes from low-cost production. Customers service is normally located in the core markets where the customers reside in order to obtain competitive advantage from the ease and speed of services. The coalignment and continuous improvement of these geographic distant processes must be established, monitored, and improved through telecommunication processes.

Several empirical studies have been conducted that indicate that appropriate coalignment (1) is a unique source of competitive advantage, (2) varies by types of product markets, (3) may depend upon the coordination of strategy between organizations, (4) can separate successful from unsuccessful multinational organizations, and (5) depends upon the continuous improvement of critical organizational linkages to remain successful.

Powell (1992) undertook a study of organizational coalignment and competitive advantage in 250 firms located in two manufacturing industries. The data revealed that "some organizational alignments do produce supernormal profits independent of the profits produced by traditional industry and strategy variables" (Powell 1992, p. 121). The author concluded that the "concept of competitive advantage need not be confined to traditional economic variables, but may be extended to such non-traditional economic variables as organizational alignment" (p. 129).

Venkatramen and Prescott (1990) undertook a study of the improvement of various organizational functions and processes and their effect upon market shares and return on investment (ROI) in seven types of markets. They classified markets into export, stable, fragmented, service, emerging, mature and declining. Employing a sample of 821 firms across a variety of industries, they tracked their continuous-improvement processes during two time periods, from 1976 to 1979 and from 1980 to 1983. Their results indicate that, depending on the type of market, some improvements in organizational functions or processes had a positive effect on market share and ROI while other improvements had a negative effect. For example, in a mature market investment intensity and increase in relative direct costs as a result of continuous-improvement programs had a negative effect accounting for 80 percent of the variance in a decline in ROI and 20 percent of the variance in a decline in market share. Conversely, a decline in compensation for workers relative to the industry and a decline in prices increased both market share and ROI. This research program suggests that continuous-improvement programs must target market specific organizational functions and business processes or suffer negative economic consequences.

Nohria and Carcia-Pont (1991) undertook a study of auto firms where portions of their value chain resided outside the organization due to external liking agreements such as joint ventures, alliances, minority holdings, etc. Exploring such linkages in the global auto industry, these authors found that between 1980 and 1990 the strategic coalignment of these firms contributed significantly to the competitive advantage obtained by the focal firm, while a lack of coalignment led to the loss of market shares (Nohria and Carcia-Pont 1991, p. 105).

Cvar (1986) attempted to determine if the rapid coalignment of a firm's internal and external sources relative to one's competitors could separate successful from unsuccessful firms in a volatile environment. Twelve industrial corporations were studied—eight successful and four unsuccessful firms across industries. Four of the successful firms were American, while one each was Swiss, British, Italian and French. Three of the four unsuccessful firms were American and one was Swiss. Successful firms were distinguished from unsuccessful by their high investment in coalignment processes which allowed a quick response to environmental changes.

Smith, Grim, Chen and Gannon (1989) questioned twenty-two top managers from high technology firms. These researchers explained major portions of the variance in organizational performance, increased profits and sales from coalignment processes. They found that an external orientation, a rapid response to competitor products, and the radicalness of the change initiated in an organization's coalignment were related to increases in organizational performance.

Our brief summary of the empirical literature has led to some significant generalizations about the continuous improvement of organizational linking or coalignment processes. This research suggests that appropriate coalignment is (1) a unique source of competitive advantage; (2) which varies positively and negatively by specific organizational functions and processes in different types of product markets; (3) which may depend upon the coalignment of aspects of the value chain residing outside the corporation; (4) which can separate successful from unsuccessful firms; and (5) which requires continuous improvement of critical organizational linkages to remain successful. Attention is now directed to the strategic and theoretic perspective governing these coalignment or linking processes.

STRATEGIC AND THEORETIC PERSPECTIVE GOVERNING COALIGNMENT OR LINKING PROCESSES

> In theory network forms allow large organizations to exist without encumbered inefficiencies of over-burdened line structures. It is worth noting, however, that network conglomerates have become feasible only in the past few years due to advances in information technologies. Thus, organizations, for the first time, have the opportunity for more dynamic horizontal and structural communication linkages. Quite possibly, only those conglomerates that utilize these new structural and communication mediums can and will survive.
>
> C. Barnett and P. Wong, "Acquisitions Activity and Organizational Structure"

From both a strategic and a theoretic perspective, the management of appropriate organizational linkages aimed at creating a strategic capability that will yield a sustainable competitive advantage is the key to organizational success in the 1990s. We will now direct attention to an explication of this key strategic and theoretic process. More specifically, we shall (1) explore the process of environmental scanning in order to locate potential sources and strategies for obtaining competitive advantage and (2) explicate a theory for converting value chain potential into strategic organizational capabilities, which, when linked to customers, will create sustainable competitive advantage.

Environmental scanning, according to Preble, Rau and Reichel is "that part of the strategic planning process in which emerging trends, changes and issues are regularly monitored and evaluated as to their likely impact on corporate decision making" (1988, p. 5). Environmental scanning usually entails (1) gathering data, (2) analyzing data, and (3) selecting a strategy.

Gathering data involves partitioning the external environment into meaningful sectors such as the industry environment, the competitive environment, and the general environment. The *industry environment* data are normally tracked in three areas: product information, market information, and customer information. Product information is scanned in three areas: products covered in the industry and the current state of each product, range of products developed recently, and technological advancement in products. Market information is gathered also in three areas: a list of markets covered in the industry, the condition of each market (i.e. emerging, saturated, etc.), and total share of market already covered. Customer information is gathered in these three areas: identification of customers and their needs, changes in their needs and habits, and geographic distribution of customers. The *competitive environment* data are normally information regarding the most threatening competitors and their market share trends and sales strategies, their technological and R&D capabilities related to competitive advantage, and their financial, technological and managerial resources. The *general environment* data are normally collected in four areas: economic information, government plans and policies, supplier information, and manpower information.

Monitoring an organization's industrial, competitive, and general environments is useful only if this information is analyzed effectively and utilized judicially.

Analyzing the data obtained in environmental scanning is at once a simple and complex process. It is simple in that the critical information required to analyze the underlying dynamics of an industry and market is frequently readily available to all the competitors. It is complex in that the number of areas monitored to affect this dynamic may be large.

Selecting a strategy is based upon a careful analysis of one's environment. A careful analysis of one's competitors involves exploring each link in a competitor's value chain to see which if any functional units and/or business processes might be a potential source of competitive advantage for either one's competitors or oneself. Once this process has been repeated for each of one's most threatening competitors, then one has a strategic outline of potential sources of competitive advantage for the industry. When this outline is complete, then a firm is in a position to select a strategy for dealing with each of its competitors. Five such strategies appear to be evident: confront, focus, circumvent, join, and withdraw.

1. *Confront.* When a value chain comparison reveals substantial competitive advantage for one's own firm at both the functional and business process level of competition, then a firm can undertake head-to-head confrontation. Toyota chose to confront Mercedes and BMW in the United States luxury car market with its Lexus car because Toyota believed it could obtain sustain-

able competitive advantage in price from each of its functions and business processes while generating quality equal to or greater than its two competitors. The results were dramatic. Toyota grabbed 23 percent of the market, all at the expense of Mercedes and BMW, while ranking lowest in customer complaints, 47 per 1,000 cars, while Mercedes had 99 per 100 and BMW had 141 per 100 ("U.S. Car Brands" 1991, p. B3).

2. *Focus.* When a value chain comparison reveals an insignificant competitive advantage at both the functional and business processes level except in one area of important concern to the customer, then one can focus upon manifesting a competitive advantage in that area. VISA Credit Card company developed an artificial intelligence system for electronically approving credit card purchases within sixty seconds. This electronic system has cut down the average store owner nonpayment of purchase slips by 82 percent per year. This saves both VISA and the stores it services billions of U.S. dollars per year. By focusing on this aspect of its value chain, VISA has been able to dramatically increase its market share while decreasing its bad debts (Feigenbaum, McCorduck, and Nii 1988).

3. *Circumvent.* When a value chain comparison reveals a substantial competitive advantage from circumventing some aspect of a competitor's value chain, then a firm can undertake head-to-head competition. Perrigo is a private drug firm that manufactures any liquid, pill or capsule that is a large seller and is off patent. It contacts major sales outlets and produces a product in the same size, shape, and color package and with the same content as a well-known brand product. However, where the brand name would normally appear, it places the name of the chain's store selling the product. Since Perrigo has no R&D costs and no advertising costs, it can market its products at a much lower cost than its brand name competitors. When the product is put on the shelf of a chain store near the brand name product, most customers can't tell the difference in package and content. The customer thus picks up the less expensive product which provides large savings to the customer as well as larger profits to the chain and Perrigo than does its brand name competitors. Perrigo, by circumventing the R&D and advertising costs of its competitors' value chain, has created a sustainable competitive advantage.

4. *Join.* When a value chain comparison reveals a substantial competitive advantage for your competitor for some aspect of their

product or all of their product, then one can form whatever type of alliance is appropriate to obtain the use of that aspect or product. General Motors (GM) found that the Japanese automakers could produce a compact car at a cost of five hundred dollars less per car than GM could. It formed a joint venture with Toyota and Mitsubishi to produce cars under the Geo brand name and sell it as its own. Today the Geo series of cars, one of GM's largest selling auto segment, is produced in that manner because GM joined with Toyota and Mitsubishi in a negotiated linking arrangement.

5. *Withdraw.* When a value chain comparison reveals a substantial competitive advantage for a firm's competitor for some aspect of a product or the total product and that competitor will not join it in any way, and it cannot circumvent that aspect or product, then the firm may withdraw its product from the market in order to preserve its own reputation for other products in the market. This withdrawal may be temporary or permanent, and it may be partial or total. Between 1985 and 1992 on at least three occasions, IBM was prepared to bring out a new product in both the workstation and PC market when its chief competitors, Sun and Compaq, brought out new products just weeks ahead of IBM that were clearly superior in performance. In each time, IBM chose to cannibalize its own product rather than weaken its reputation. IBM thus took the loss in R&D and manufacturing investment rather than place a significantly inferior product on the market. In each case, the company's withdrawal was temporary, lasting until it could develop a better product (Bryan 1990).

Once a firm has developed an outline of all its competitors' value chains and analyzed its strategic position relative to each of them, then it is in a position to determine how to theoretically and practically convert its value chain potential into a strategic capability, which, when linked with customers, will create a sustainable competitive advantage.

CONVERTING VALUE CHAIN POTENTIAL INTO STRATEGIC ORGANIZATIONAL CAPABILITIES AND SUSTAINABLE COMPETITIVE ADVANTAGE

According to Coyne, sustainable competitive advantage exists when "1. customers perceive a consistent difference in important attributes between the producer's product or service and those of his competitors. 2. That difference is the direct consequence of a capability gap between the producer and his competitors. 3. Both the difference in important attributes and the capability gap can be expected to endure over time" (Coyne 1986, p. 55). A capability, according to Stalk, Evans and Shulman, "is a set of business processes strategically understood. Every company has business processes that deliver value to the customer. But few think of them as that primary object of strategy" (1992, p. 62).

Capability-based competitors review their value chain in comparison to their competitors and locate those functional and business processes in which they have competitive advantage and then try to link or coalign those functions and processes in some systematic way so as to set an industry benchmark that will yield a sustainable competitive advantage. We believe there are three separate and yet combinable theoretic means for converting value-added organizational functions and business processes into strategic capabilities that can establish a world-class benchmark and generate a sustainable competitive advantage. Those are: (1) knowledge-based coalignment, (2) alliance-based coalignment, (3) technology-based coalignment, and (4) a combination-based coalignment of value-added functions and business processes. Let us explore each in turn.

Knowledge-based Capabilities

In comparing a firm's value chain with the value chain of all of the firm's competitors, one may locate some single or combination of value-added organizational functions and/or business processes in which on excels in comparison to one's competitors. The question will then arise as to how the firm should strategically link and configure those value-added activities with its customers in order to obtain a sustainable competitive advantage. In such cases, it is one's own firm's unique knowledge in the form of value-added activities that when grouped into capabilities in linking with the customers, yields a competitive advantage. Then through the judious use of a firm's continuous-improvement program these capabilities are focused, linked, and improved in such a manner to create a sustainable competitive advantage and new world-class benchmark.

The Toyota Production System (TPS), sometimes called "lean production management," illustrates the development of such an internal knowledge-based capability. Kiichiro Toyoda and Taiichi Ohno led the development of this knowledge based capability. In the 1960s, Toyota took the skills of its automotive craftsmen and the standardization and mass-production techniques used by Ford Motor Corporation and asked their workers to form small self-managed and cross-functional teams and integrate these two processes. The goal was to combine the quality of a craftsman with the standardization of mass production. Kiichiro Toyoda also felt that each worker on this new line should be trained in several areas: production tasks, maintenance, recordkeeping, quality control, and so forth (Taylor 1990).

Management delegated to workers both the right and the responsibility to continuously improve the process. Next, Toyota formed small cross-functional teams between factory workers and suppliers in order to improve the quality and inventory levels of parts. In what must be considered a breakthrough in creative thinking, these continuous-improvement teams came with the *kanban* system. Parts were to be inspected at the manufacturer's plants and then shipped to Toyota just in time for use. This in turn substantially reduced the capital tied up in inventory, substantially reducing costs; increased the turnover ratio on capital; and substantially improved product quality (Womack, Jones, and Roos 1990a).

In the 1980s, Toyota attempted to develop a continuous-flow manufacturing system for turning out small numbers of different cars at a low price. The central problem in achieving this goal was the tooling cost and time custom-designed dies needed to stamp out parts for a car. The tools and machines needed for this stamping process form up to 73 percent of the total cost of a new car. It also accounts for two-thirds of the time needed to build a car. Cross-functional teams and self-managed teams were set up and, employing international benchmarking against the U.S. auto industry, in just three years were able to cut the cost and time of designing and manufacturing with these dies by between one-half to two-thirds when compared to the U.S. automakers.

Production processes were simplified and redesigned, and the quality was improved. Next Toyota saw the need to reorganize its management system and become more responsible by cutting out two layers of middle management—about one thousand executives. Finally, Toyota divided its product development teams into three groups: (1) small front-wheel-drive cars, (2) big rear-wheel-drive cars, and (3) trucks. In a creative breakthrough aimed at correctly targeting its specific auto models within the three divisions to narrow customer niches, each model was given a chief engineer, who headed a cross-functional team made up of representatives from each functional unit and business process in the value chain. This group scans the customers, competitors, and general economic trends in order to appropriately design, manufacture, and market a new car for its customer niche (Cusumano 1988).

After forty years of developing focused continuous-improvement programs by employing self-managed and cross-functional teams, benchmarking, and breakthroughs, Toyota's lean manufacturing system has become a model for sequencing the value-added aspects of a firm's value chain to form a knowledge based strategic capability that has created a sustainable competitive advantage. Today, Toyota builds cars and trucks on average faster, with higher quality and more unique features, and at a lower cost than any of its competitors. Customers have responded to this knowledge-based capability by increasing Toyota's market share, ranking these cars top in quality and demanding that other producers provide similar standard features (Womack, Jones, and Roos 1990).

Whereas knowledge-based capabilities reside totally in the linkages within the firm—as does the effective use of continuous-improvement programs—alliance-based capabilities reside in the negotiated linkages between firms, and so does the effective use of continuous-improvement programs.

Alliance-based Capabilities

In comparing a firm's value chain with the firm's competitors, one may find that while aspects of a firm's value chain can produce value-added activities, some portions of the firm's value chain of most concern to the customer are not present or are not functioning at an appropriate level. Under such conditions, an organization may choose to form one or more linking arrangements with other firms that are performing well in these customer-sensitive areas in order to obtain sustainable competitive advantage.

The knowledge necessary to do this resides in an alliance based strategic capability. Such linkages may take the form of mergers, acquisitions, equity partnerships, consortia, joint ventures, development agreements, supply agreements and/or marketing agreements (Nohria and Garcia-Pont 1991, p. 105). However, in all cases continuous-improvement programs are needed to set up the inside, outside, and between organization linkages and to upgrade their collective performance to create a world-class benchmark.

Successful strategic alliances are few because of the difficult problems involved in a firm having an important part of its value chain residing either partially or completely within another organization. The Ford Motor Corporation's thirteen-year joint venture with the Mazda Corporation, however, did establish world-class benchmarks for both organizations in two different areas and as such warrants our close attention.

In 1979, Ford and Mazda Corporations formed a joint venture to cooperate on the development of new vehicles and to share valuable expertise. Ford was to share product design, international marketing, and finance expertise with Mazda, while Mazda was to share product development and manufacturing expertise with Ford. Both firms were to remain totally autonomous in this joint venture. They were to undertake only those cooperative projects that offered mutual benefits. This was to be judged on a project-by-project basis. Early on, the need for a set of operating rules, a set of coordination rules, and an impartial outside arbitrator for disputes became evident. Mazda and Ford outlined those operating rules.

> 1. **Keep top management involved:** The boss must set a tone for the relationship. Otherwise middle managers will resist ceding partial control of a project to a partner.
>
> 2. **Meet often, and often informally:** Meeting should be at all levels and should include time for socializing. Trust can't be built solely around a boardroom table.
>
> 3. **Use a matchmaker:** A third party can mediate disputes, suggest new ways of approaching the partner, and offer an independent sounding board.
>
> 4. **Maintain your independence:** Independence helps both parties hone the areas of expertise that made them desirable partners in the first place.
>
> 5. **Allow no "sacrifice" deals:** Every project must be viable for each partner. It is up to senior management to see that an overall balance is maintained.

6. **Appoint a monitor:** Someone must take primary responsibility for monitoring all aspects of the alliance.

7. **Anticipate cultural differences:** They may be corporate, or national. Stay flexible, and try to place cultrally sensitive executives in key posts. (Treece, Miller, and Melcher 1992, p. 104)

A four-man monitoring group was then set up, and it established coordination rules. Members of this group come in daily contact with each other by computer and must meet face to face at least once every eight months. Four months after this group's face-to-face meeting, Ford's and Mazda's chairmen and staff meet to review the progress of ongoing projects. Also, twice each year the heads of each firm's product development and manufacturing units meet. In addition, self-managed, cross-functional, international benchmarking teams for each project work together daily (p. 104).

Finally, a member of the Sumitomo Bank of Japan was selected as the impartial arbitrator for unresolvable disputes. Such disputes arose frequently in the early years of the joint venture and then disappeared entirely (p. 103). Ford and Mazda's joint venture has helped each firm establish world-class organizational capabilities in previously weak areas of their respective value chains. For example, today one in every four cars sold in the United States has benefitted from some degree of Mazda's help, while two of every five Mazdas have had some Ford help. In addition, Ford obtained access to Mazda's distribution capabilities in Japan and became the largest American seller, 72,000 of U.S. cars in Japan in 1991, and modeled its super efficient Hermosilla, Mexico plant on the design of a Mazda plant in Japan (p. 103). Today, thanks to Mazda, Ford's Mexico manufacturing plant is outpacing all other U.S. and Japanese corporations in reducing product cost and increasing product quality (Lohr 1992, p. D2). The Mazda-Ford alliance has led to a dramatic increase in Mazda's auto market shares (Treece, Miller, and Melcher 1992, p. 104).

Technology-based Capabilities

In comparing a firm's value chain with its competitors, one may find that while some aspects of a firm's value chain can produce value-added activities, some portions of its value chain of most concern to the customers cannot do so without the addition of some new state-of-the-art technology. Under such conditions, the firm's entire value chain may be in need of modification in order to reap the benefits of the addition of this new technology.

The knowledge necessary to obtain this value-added advantage resides in the innovative and appropriate use of these new technologies. In all cases, continuous-improvement programs are necessary to implement the new technologies and to appropriately adjust the value chain to the technology so as not to lose other value-added gains. The corporations that have attempted to leapfrog their competition but failed to do so are legion, including GM, IBM and AT&T. However, one such attempt that has led to dramatic success is that of The Limited.

The Limited Company is a major manufacturer of women's apparel throughout the world. Each evening the store managers in thirty-two hundred stores across the United States collect data regarding sales for that day—size, color, fashion number, and so forth—through their electronic point of sale computer system (EPOS). The cutting order information is telecommunicated to The Limited's workshops in Hong Kong, Singapore, and Sri Lanka, and it is translated into the next day's manufacturing orders. Within days these just-in-time inventory replacements are shipped to The Limited's Ohio distribution center on a Boeing 747.

In addition to supplying replacement merchandise in a timely fashion, The Limited's EPOS system can be used to monitor marketing. It can track fashion design performance, pinpointing age groups, income level, and geographic locations where specific fashion designs sell well. Ultimately, EPOS could be used for ordering customized designs by color, size, cut, and style with less than one week turnaround on delivery of orders. In the use of electronic point of sale merchandising for customized design, computer integrated manufacturing for production, and just-in-time product delivery for marketing, we see R&D, marketing, and manufacturing fused into a flexible, high-speed, reciprocally coordinated interface system (Phillips and Dunkin 1989, p. 192).

The Limited has diversified its business in 1990 by acquiring Lerner, Victoria's Secret, and Lane Bryant and by opening The Limited Express. Each of these chains has employed EPOS as a value-added tool for successfully dominating its respective market niche (p. 199).

Finally, "The Limited's mass merchandisers can take the newest trends from Paris or New York and place cheaper versions in its stores weeks before the original designs are produced"

(Hochswender 1990, p. 5). This provides The Limited with a technology based capability for dominating its respective markets.

Combination-based Coalignment

In comparing a firm's value chain with that of its competitors, one may find that while some aspects of the firm's value chain can produce value-added activities, many other portions of utmost customer concern cannot do so without linking with other firms in order to obtain some knowledge-based, some alliance-based, and some technology-based capabilities. In such cases, the focal organization may enter into numerous linking arrangements between parts of its own organization and parts of others in order to capitalize on the value-added activities of all the firms.

IBM recently experienced its first loss of income in more than fifty years. In an effort to respond quickly to these losses and become more profitable, IBM decentralized its management system, cut personnel, and allowed the decentralized organizations to enter into alliances with other firms in an attempt to strengthen their core capabilities.

In an attempt to increase their knowledge-based, alliance-based, and technology-based core capabilities, IBM entered into four types of alliances. Knowledge-based alliances or strategic alliances were formed with Stratus, Motorola, Apple, Novell, Borland, Lotus, AT&T, and Systems Application Architecture. Technology based alliances were formed with Motorola, Compaq, Apple, Intel, Sybase, Borland, Lotus, and Systems Application Architecture. Alliance-based relationships were formed through equity partnerships and joint ventures with Microsoft over Microsoft Windows program, which competed directly with IBM's 052. IBM is currently involved in more than one thousand negotiated linking arrangements with other firms, arrangements aimed at enhancing all its core capabilities.

In conclusion, capability-based competitors review their value chain in comparison to their competitors and locate those functional and business processes in which they have competitive advantage and then try to link or coalign those functions or processes in some systematic way so as to set world-class benchmarks that will yield sustainable competitive advantage through knowledge-based, alliance-based, technology-based, and combination-based coalignment. Continuous-improvement programs are then employed to generate and maintain this sustainable competitive advantage. Toyota, Ford, and The Limited each in turn employed capabilities analysis as outlined above successfully to obtain a recognizable sustainable competitive advantage.

CHAPTER 8

Looking into Tomorrow

> For two hundred years people have founded and built companies around Adam Smith's brilliant discovery that industrial work should be broken down into its simplest and most basic *tasks*. In the postindustrial business age we are now entering, corporations will be founded and built around the idea of reunifying those tasks into coherent business *processes*.
> S. Hammer and J. Champy, *Reengineering the Corporation*

As we conclude our brief but concept-packed journey, we wish to go back, ideawise, to where we started to remind our readers of two very important ideas regarding organizational teamwork. First, teamwork is one of the most important communication processes and tools through and with which to come up with a firm's sustaining competitive advantage in order to survive and thrive in a volatile, ever-changing business environment; you can't go very far without sincerely and effectively employing some of the fundamental teamwork concepts and skills to handle the external contingencies and internal complexities in modern business life. Teamwork can be magic. Second, an equally important idea is the one that teamwork has its serious limitations either in a normal organizational context or in a high-speed management environment, whether or not barriers are removed in the process; teamwork offers no panacea for all modern organizational ills or problems. Under certain circumstances, something worse could happen: teamwork, which has been magic for your competitors or was once magic for your own firm, could become a management disaster that could bring the organization to complete collapse.

First, teamwork can be magic.

It can be magic if the use of it is appropriately contextualized. It is in the context of high-speed management that we discuss the various concepts, processes, and characteristics of organizational teamwork. It is a fundamental requirement that those who use teamwork understand the nature of such a context. They need to understand that the high-speed management philosophy as a set of communication principles, strategies, and tools is the only effective response to the dynamics created as a result of, firstly, the still-evolving information and communication revolution, secondly, the emergence of a global economy and the three core markets with rapid increases in international trade, and thirdly, a volatile business climate characterized by rapidly changing technology, shrinking product life cycles, and quick market saturation. Such dynamics in the global, national, and regional economies call for an organizational management system that is innovative, adaptive, flexible, efficient, and extremely responsive. Only when a firm understands the nature of the current environmental context can it understand and be capable of using teamwork in a creative way to help sustain competitive advantage. Only then can teamwork have the potential to become magic.

Teamwork can be magic if the use of it is based on a profound understanding of the interdependent nature of modern organizational life in the context of high-speed management. The increasingly competitive external environment and mounting internal organizational complexities have rendered it insufficient for firms to marginally recognize and tactically manage the interdependencies of intra- as well as interorganizational variables. The understanding and execution of such interdependencies must be raised to a higher and strategic level. The value chain theory, which we discussed in chapters 2 and 7, should help us gain such an understanding. We want to emphasize, at the very end of this conceptual journey of ours, that teamwork is the very communication process with which to manage modern intra- and interorganizational interdependencies, both tactically and strategically. Teamwork viewed as such is the use of information and communication to coalign all organizational resources available for use along the value chain of an organization or the value system between organizations to create competitive advantage. In this sense, teamwork as a communication process is closest to the concept of 'organizational interdependencies' on the conceptual map of an organization or interorganizational field. And this is why teamwork can be magic for organizational success.

Teamwork can be magic if it is used to achieve the goal of speed-to-market based on international benchmarking within the framework of high-speed management. One can hardly find a book or article that talks about teamwork without talking about goals as one of the most important success factors of organizational teamwork. Everyone knows that having a goal is important for a group if it is to move up, qualitatively, to become a team. In the framework of high-speed management, given all the reasons we analyzed in previous chapters, and in chapter 3 in particular, teams, whatever their type, must keep speed-to-market as their ultimate goal to achieve. A high-performance team constantly asks itself whether it is contributing or setting barriers to the overall organizational goal of speed-to-market. And all its members are fully aware of the meaning of speed in a high-speed management environment: when you have it, you survive and prosper; when you lack it, you suffer and die. In order to jointly contribute to the achieving of the overall goal of speed-to-market, a team in a high-speed management firm must also set for itself specific, short-term goals. An internationally, nationally, or regionally competitive firm and its teams would perform international benchmarking to locate the best practices in its industry or particular field. In this sense, teamwork in a high-performance organization is always an inseparable part of its continuous-improvement programs. Understandably, the magic of teamwork comes partly from a team's commitment to its general goal of speed-to-market and specific task goals based on international benchmarking.

Teamwork can be magic if a firm's over-layered structure is simplified, its many rules and regulations is melted into team culture, and team members' role definitions become more fluid and flexible. An over-layered organizational structure, excessive organizational rules and regulations, rigid reporting relationships, strict division of labor, and rigid definitions of role responsibilities—legacies of the industrial revolution—worked in Adam Smith's times but have gradually become killers of efficiency, quick response to market needs, and in the end, the corporate life of those organizations that were too slow to change. Teamwork can proceed effectively only when such killers are themselves sentenced to die. Only then can team members cross functional lines easily, free themselves from rigid role confinement, and become part of what Hammer and Champy call a coherent business "process" in this chapter's epigraph (Hammer and Champy 1993, p. 2).

Teamwork can be magic if team members possess the qualities of intensity, permanent dissatisfaction, effective and speedy communication, and consistency, which are needed to handle the toughness of a highly competitive, highly complex high-speed environment. Not all organization members are born qualified team players. It takes training to transform an individual organizational member to a committed team player. For a team to perform effectively in an organization that follows high-speed management principles, it requires a high level of energy and commitment on the part of its team members (intensity). Commitment generates and maintains team spirit, and high commitment inspires high team spirit, which is essential for a high-performance team. They should also vigorously involve themselves in the firm's as well as in their team's continuous-improvement programs (permanent dissatisfaction). Part of the magic of teamwork comes from the belief on the part of team players that nothing is so good that can no longer be improved upon. And they must know how to communicate speedily and effectively with all stakeholders both inside and outside the organization (speedy and effective communication). As we indicated previously, high-speed management depends on high-speed communication, high-speed sharing of information among team members, and then high-speed problem solving. Lastly, team members must remain consistent in their pursuit of excellence (consistency). Satisfying these four member qualitative conditions works the magic of solving the tough problems that may arise in a high-speed environment.

Teamwork can be magic if a team and its team members know how to anchor and reanchor themselves in organizational life structurally, culturally, psychologically, and in regard to mastery of skills. They should do so in a way that helps the team develop mutually constructed and publicly agreed to or shared goals; appropriately integrates the team's members by addressing their unique interests, concerns, and contributions to that shared goal; and generates such behaviors as mutual respect, trust, and confidence that combine to lead to team synergy. Structurally, team members must solidly anchor themselves in their "core competency" and outsource the rest those that other companies do better and more cheaply. Culturally, there must be a fit between the values that an organization collectively holds and the values that an individual team member privately adheres to. Psychologically, needs compatibility must be worked out between the organization and individual team members. As far as work skills are concerned, workers in a high-speed management firm are supposed to be trained in a multiskilling system where each learns to perform the jobs of others as well as his or her own. Research indicates that having the four anchorages could help develop mutually agreed to goals, integrate team components, and promote teamwork values, which is where the magic of teamwork is hidden (see chapter 1).

Yes, teamwork can be magic, and that is why we have worked on this book.

But teamwork is no panacea.

Indeed there is no such thing as a panacea for curing all organizational ills and problems. Teamwork, like other communication or management tools, has its own limitations, and under certain circumstances such limitations may be quite negative and destructive. Let's name a few. *First*, teamwork may simply become a management gimmick if the above six "if" conditions are not satisfied. We suggest that if a firm is not quite prepared for meeting the above "if" conditions, it not talk about teamwork. *Second*, there will be no teamwork if team leadership is missing. It is largely a fantasy to think that the mere fact that a group of people are put together generates teamwork. Leadership is always needed, even in self-managing teams where leadership tends to be "distributed" among team members. Lack of team leadership may lead to total chaos. *Third*, there tends to be a strong correlation between the successful use of different types of teamwork and the overall competency levels of an organization as reflected in general ROA-based profitability and VAE-based productivity levels (for a review of the idea, see table 1.2). A mismatch between the two will have a less or no chance to succeed. *Fourth*, some work simply gets done faster and better with one person instead of with a team, whether or not it is done in a high-speed management environment. Understandably, in some high-speed environment situations, one single person alone can work magic; teamwork may well delay an action and create an opportunity-losing experience. When one person is capable of working more efficiently and effectively under certain conditions, why use teamwork?

As we complete our journey and look into tomorrow, we are worried and thrilled. We are worried because tomorrow is even more uncertain than today, and we are by no means sure regarding the extent to which the theories, concepts, and other conceptual tools we have discussed here in this book can work in a changed and still changing environment. We are thrilled, because uncertainties mean opportunities, opportunities not only for organizations, new and old, but also for teams and team members, middle managers, front line workers, and us organizational researchers. The number of opportunities for conceptual recreation and practical reexperimentation are just phenomenal.

Tomorrow's organizations are organizations that will be fundamentally different from the ones that were created during the Industrial Revolution and even significantly different from the ones that are currently in the process of their recreation. They will be more innovative, more adaptive, more flexible, more efficient, and more responsive to market needs if they are the ones that survive. There will be one thing that all organizations of tomorrow will share, and that is a sense of the importance of the role that teamwork will play in a high-speed business environment. It is no panacea, but it can work magic if properly used, today and even more so tomorrow.

REFERENCES

Altany, P. (1990). "Copycats." *Industry Week* 242 (Nov. 5), pp. 11–18.
———. (1991). "Share and Share Alike." *Industry Week* 240 (July 15), pp. 12–17.
———. (1992). "Benchmarkers Unite." *Industry Week* 241 (Feb. 3), p. 1.
Ancona, D., and D. A. Nadler. (1989). "Top Hats and Executive Tales: Designing the Senior Team." *Sloan Management Review* (fall), pp. 19–28.
Anderson, P. F. (1981). "Marketing Investment Analysis." In J. N. Sheth, ed., *Research in Marketing* 4. Greenwich, Conn.: JAI Press.
Baig, E. (1989). "Where Global Growth Is Going." *Fortune* (July 13), pp. 71–88.
Barnett, C., and P. Wong. (1992). "Acquisitions Activity and Organizational Structure." *Journal of General Management* 17(3) (spring), pp. 1–15.
Barrett, F. D. (1987). "Teamwork: How to Expand Its Power and Punch." *Business Quarterly* 52(3), pp. 24–31.
Barry, D. (1991). "Managing Bossless Team: Lessons in Distributed Leadership." *Organizational Dynamics* 20(1), pp. 31–47.
"Benchmarking: How Companies Learn from the Best to Become the Best." (1992) *National Report* (July–Aug.), p. 1.
Berlant, D., R. Browning, and G. Foster. (1990). "How Hewlett-Packard Gets Numbers It Can Trust." *Harvard Business Review* (Jan.–Feb.), pp. 178–182.
Bolman, L. G., and T. E. Deal. (1992). "What Makes a Team Work?" *Organizational Dynamics* 21(2), pp. 34–44.
Borrus, A. (1990). "Japanese Streak Ahead in Asia." *Business Week* (May 7), pp. 54–55.
Bryan, E. (1990). "The World Turned Upside Down? IBM in the 1990s." *Business Horizons* (Nov.–Dec.), pp. 39–47.
Camp, R. (1992). "Learning from the Best Leads to Superior Performance." *Journal of Business Strategy* (July), pp. 3–5.
Castells, M. (1986). "High-Technology, World Development and the Structured Transformations: The Trends and Debate." *Alternatives* 11, pp. 297–342.
Clare, D. A., and D. G. Sanford. (1984). "Cooperation and Conflict between Industrial Sales and Production." *Industrial Marketing Management* 13, pp. 163–69.

Cohen, B. P., and X. Zhan (1991). "Status Processes in Enduring Work Group. " *American Sociological Review* 56 (Apr. 1), pp. 79–188.

Coyne, K. (1986). "Sustainable Competitive Advantage—What It Is, What It Isn't." *Business Horizons* (Jan.–Feb.), pp. 54–61.

Cushman, D. P. "The Crack, in Quality." (1992).*The Economist* (Apr. 18), pp. 67–68.

———. (1993). "When Is Teamwork a Good and When Is It a Bad Solution to Organizational Problems?" In M. Cross and W. Cummins, eds., *Approaching 2000, Proceedings of the Sixth Conference on Corporate Communication* (Rutherford, N.J.: Fairleigh Dickinson University), pp. 83–89.

Cushman, D. P., and S. S. King. (1984). "The Role of Communication in High Technology Organizations: The Emergence of High-Speed Management." In S. S. King, ed., *Human Communication as a Field of Study*. Albany: SUNY Press.

———. (1993). "Visions of Order: High-Speed Management in the Private Sector of the Global Marketplace." In A. Kozminski and D. P. Cushman, eds., *Organizational Communication and Management: A Global Perspective*. Albany: SUNY Press.

———. (1994a). *High-speed Management and Organizational Communication in the 1990s*. Albany: SUNY Press.

———. (1994b). "High-Speed Management as a Theoretic Principle for Yielding Significant Organizational Communication Behaviors." In B. Kovacic, ed., *New Approaches to Organizational Communication: A Reader*. Albany: SUNY Press.

Cusumano, M. A. (1985). *The Japanese Automobile Industry*. Cambridge: Harvard University Press.

———. (1988). "Manufacturing Innovation: Lessons from the Japanese Auto Industry." *Sloan Management Review* (fall), pp. 29–39.

Cvar, M. (1986). "Case Studies in Global Competition Patterns of Success and Failure." In M. Porter, ed., *Competition in Global Industry*. Boston: Harvard Business School Press.

Dumaine, B. (1989). "How Managers Can Succeed through Speed." *Fortune* (Feb. 13), pp. 54–59.

———. (1991). "The Bureaucracy Busters." *Fortune* (June 17), pp. 36–50.

———. (1993). "The New Non-Manager Managers" *Fortune* (Feb. 22), pp. 80–84.

Emery, F., and E. Trist. (1960). "Sociotechnical Systems." In C. W. Churchman and M. Verhurst, eds., *Management Science, Models, and Techniques*. Elmsford, NY: Pergamon Press.

Feder, B. (1993). "At Motorola, Quality Is a Team Sport." *New York Times* (Jan. 21), p. D1.

Feigenbaum, E., P. McCorduck, and P. Nii. (1988). *The Rise of the Expert Company*. New York: Times Books.

Feschetti, M. (1987). "The Global Automobile: Banishing the Necktie." *IEEE Spectrum* 24, pp. 50–52.

Fiorelli, J. (1988). "Power in Work Groups: Team Members' Perspectives." *Human Relations* 41(1), pp. 1–12.

Flint, J. (1991). "Banza: With a Georgia Accent." *Forbes* (Feb. 4), pp. 58–60.

Flynn, R., T. McCombs, and D. Elloy. (1990). "Staffing the Self-Managing Work Team." *Leadership & Organizational Development Journal* 11(1), pp. 26–31.

Fraker, S. (1984). "High-Speed Management for the High Tech Age." *Fortune* (Feb. 13), pp. 34–60.

Fuchberg, G. (1992a). "Quality Programs Show Shoddy Results." *Wall Street Journal* (Oct. 1), p. B1.

———. (1992b). "Total Quality Is Termed Only a Partial Success." *Wall Street Journal* (Oct. 1), p. B1.

Geertz, C. (1978). "The Bazaar Economy: Information and Search in Peasant Marketing." *American Economic Review*, supplement, pp. 28–32.

"The Global Giants." (1990). *Wall Street Journal* (Sept. 21), p. R27.

Gupta, A. K., and D. Wileman. (1988). "The Credibility-Cooperation Connection at the R&D-Marketing Interface." *Journal of Product Innovation Management* 5, pp. 20–31.

Hackman, J. R., and G. R. Oldham. (1980). *Work Redesign*. Reading, Mass.: Addison-Wesley.

Hackman, J. R., G. R. Oldham, R. Janson, and K. Purdy. (1975). "A New Strategy for Job Enrichment." *California Management Review* 17(4), pp. 55–71.

Hall, E. T. (1991). "Context and Meaning." In L. A. Samovar and R. E. Porter, eds., *Intercultural Communication: A Reader*. Belmont, Calif.: Wadsworth Publishing Company.

Hammer, M., and J. Champy. (1993). *Reengineering the Corporation: A Manifesto for Business Revolution*. New York: HarperCollins Publishers.

Hochi, S. (1986). "Japanese Auto Companies: At Home in America." *Business Japan* 31, pp. 24–29.

Hochswender, W. (1990). "How Fashion Spreads Around the World at the Speed of Light." *New York Times* (May 13), p. E5.

Hoerr, J. (1989). "The Payoff from Teamwork." *Business Week* (July 10), pp. 56–62.

Huey, J. (1991). "Nothing Is Impossible." *Fortune* (Sept. 23), pp. 135–40.

Jennings, K., and F. Westfall. (1992). "Benchmarking for Strategic Action." *Journal of Business Strategy* (July), pp. 22–25.

Kanter, R. (1989). "Becoming Pals: Pooling, Allying and Linking Across Companies." *The Academy of Management Executive* 3 (3), pp. 183–93.
Kelley, R. (1989). "In Praise of Followers." *Harvard Business Review* (Nov.–Dec.), pp. 142–47.
Kendrick, J. (1992). "Benchmarking Survey Builds Case for Looking to Others for TQM Models." *Quality* (Mar.), p. 1.
King, S., and D. Cushman, ed. (1994). *High-Speed Management and Organizational Communication in the 1990s: A Reader*. Albany: SUNY Press.
Kinlaw, D. C. (1991). *Developing Superior Work Teams*. San Diego: Lexington Books, University Associates.
Kolodny, H. F., and B. Dresner. (1986). "Linking Arrangements and New Work Design." *Organizational Dynamics* 14(3), pp. 33–51.
Kovacic, B. (1992). "High-Speed Management, Environmental Scanning, and Coalignment of External Resources: Strategic Alliances." In M. Cross and W. Cummins, eds., *Proceedings of the Fifth Conference on Corporate Communication: Communication in Uncertain Times*. Madison, N.J.: Fairleigh Dickinson University.
Kreps, G. L. (1990). *Organizational Communication: Theory and Practice* (2nd ed.), New York: Longman.
Lefton, R. E., and V. R. Buzzotta. (1987–88). "Teams and Teamwork: A Study of Executive-Level Teams." *National Productivity Review* (winter), pp. 7–19.
Lohr, S. (1992). "Ford and Chrysler Outpace Japanese in Reducing Costs." *New York Times* (June 18), p. D2.
Lucas, G. H., and A. J. Bush. (1988). "The Marketing-R&D Interface: Do Personality Factors Have an Impact?" *Journal of Product Innovation Management* 5, pp. 257–68.
Main, J. (1992). "How to Steal the Best Ideas Around." *Fortune* (Oct. 19), pp. 102–6.
Miles, R., and C. Snow. (1984). "Fit, Failure and the Hall of Fame." *California Management Review* 26(3), pp. 10–28.
Nicholls, J. R. (1985). "An Alloplastic Approach to Corporate Culture." *International Studies of Man and Organization* 14(4), pp. 32–63.
Nohria, N., and C. Garcia-Pont. (1991). "Global Strategic Linkages and Industrial Structure." *Strategic Management Journal* 12, pp. 105–24.
Noj, A. K. (1993). "G.E. First Quarter Profits Rose 10 percent; Earning Exceed Analysts' Estimate." *Wall Street Journal* (Apr. 14), p. A4.
Ouchi, W. G. (1981). *Theory Z*. New York: Avon Books.
Pepper, C. B. (1989). "Fast Forward." *Business Month* (Feb.), pp. 25–30.
Peters, T. (1987). *Thriving on Chaos*. New York: Harper and Row.

Phillips, S., and A. Dunkin. (1989). "Is There No Limit to The Limited's Growth?" *Business Week* (Nov. 8), pp. 192–99.

Pinto, M. B., and J. K. Pinto. (1990). "Project Team Communication and Cross-functional Cooperation in New Program Development." *Journal of Product Innovation Management* 7, pp. 200–11.

Poling, H. (1989). "An Interview with the CEO Designate of Ford Motors Company." *Automotive News* (Nov. 7), p. E8.

Port, O. (1986). "High Tech to the Rescue." *Business Week* (June 16), pp. 100–108.

———. (1992). "Beg, Borrow and Benchmark." *Business Week* (Nov. 30), pp. 74–75.

Port, O., J. Cary, K. Kelley, and S. Forest. (1992). "Quality." *Business Week* (Nov. 30), pp. 66–72.

Powell, T. (1992). "Organizational Alignment as Competitive Advantage." *Strategic Management Journal* 13, pp. 119–34.

Preble, J., P. Rau, and A. Reichel. (1988). "The Environmental Scanning Practices of U.S. Multinationals in the Late 1990s." *Management Information Review* 28(4), pp. 4–14.

Quickel, S. W. (1990). "Welch on Welch." *Financial World* 159(7), pp. 62–70.

Reese, J. (1993). "America's Most Admired Corporations." *Fortune* (Feb. 8), pp. 44–72.

Rockart, J., and J. Short. (1989). "IT in the 1990s: Managing Organizational Interdependence." *Sloan Management Review* (winter), pp. 7–17.

Ruffin, W. (1990). "Wired for Speed." *Business Month* (Jan.), pp. 56–58.

Russell, E., A. Adams, and B. Boundy. (1986). "High-Technology Test Marketing Campbell Soup Company." *Journal of Consumer Marketing* 3, pp. 71–80.

Saski, T. (1991). "How the Japanese Accelerated New Car Development." *Long Range Planning* 24(1), pp. 15–25.

Scarr, L. (1992). "Intrepid Wears 'LH' Label like a Winner." *San Diego Union Tribune* (Dec. 22), p. A1.

Schmidt, A. (1992). "How Blue Chips Stock Up. " *Fortune* (Nov. 30), p. 16.

Schoemaker, P. (1992). "How to Link Strategic Vision to Core Capabilities." *Sloan Management Review* (fall), pp. 67–81.

Schroeder, D., and A. Robinson. (1991). "America's Most Successful Export to Japan:Continuous Improvement Programs." *Sloan Management Review* (spring), pp. 67–81.

Sherman, S. (1992). "Are Strategic Alliances Working?" *Fortune* (Sept. 21), pp. 72–78.

Smith, K.G., C. M. Grimm, M. J. Chen, and M. J. Gannon. (1989). "Predictors of Response Time to Competitive Strategic Action: Preliminary Theory and Evidence." *Journal of Business Research* 19, pp. 245–58.

Stalk, G., Jr. (1988). "Time: The Next Source of Competitive Advantage." *Harvard Business Review* (July–Aug.), pp. 41–51.
Stalk, G., P. Evans, and L. Shulman. (1992). "Competing on Capabilities: The New Role of Corporate Strategy." *Harvard Business Review* (Mar.–Apr.), pp. 57–69.
Stewart, T. (1991). "GE Keeps Those Ideas Coming." *Fortune* (Aug. 12), pp. 41–49.
Taylor, A., III. (1990a). "Can American Cars Come Back?" *Fortune* (Feb. 26), pp. 62–65.
———. (1990b). "Why Toyota Keeps Getting Better and Better and Better." *Fortune* (Nov. 19), pp. 66–79.
Taylor, J. C., and R. A. Asadorian. (1985). "The Implementation of Excellence: STS Management." *Industrial Management* 27 (4), pp. 5–15.
Tichy, N., and R. Charzon. (1989). "Speed, Simplicity, and Self-Confidence: An Interview with Jack Welch." *Harvard Business Review* (Sept.–Oct.), pp. 112–20.
Toyoda, J. (1988). *Toyota: A History of the First 50 Years*. Toyota Motor Corporation.
Treece, J. (1990). "How Ford and Mazda Shared the Driver's Seat." *Business Week* (Mar. 26), pp. 94–95.
Treece, J., and J. Howr. (1989). "Shaking Up. " *Business Week* (Aug. 14), pp. 24–80.
Treece, J., L. Miller, and R. Melcher. (1992). "The Partners." *Business Week* (Feb. 10), pp. 102–7.
Tully, S. (1993). "The Modular Corporation." *Fortune* (Feb. 8), pp. 106–15.
"U.S. Car Brands Improve Quality." (1991). *USA Today* (June 3), p. B3.
Venkatraman, N., and J. Prescott. (1990). "Environment-Strategy Coalignment: An Empirical Test of Its Performance Implications." *Strategic Management Journal* 11, pp. 1–23.
Vesey, J. T. (1991). "The New Competitors: They Think in Terms of Speed-to-Market." *Academy of Management Executive* 5(2), pp. 22–33.
"The Virtual Organization." *Business Week* (Feb. 8, 1993), pp. 99–102.
Walton, J. (1985). "The IMF Riot." Paper delivered at the ISA Conference on the Urban Impact of the New International Division of Labor, Hong Kong.
Weatherly, J. (1992). "Dare to Compare for Better Productivity." *HR Magazine* (Sept.), pp. 59–64.
Wellins, R., and J. George. (1991). "The Key to Self-Directed Teams." *Training & Development Journal* 45(4) (Apr.), pp. 26–31.
White, J. (1991). "Japanese Auto Makers Help U.S. Suppliers Become More Efficient." *Wall Street Journal* (Sept. 9), pp. A1, A7.

Wiesamdanger, B. (1992). "Benchmarking for Beginners." *Sales and Marketing Management* (Nov.), pp. 59–64.

Womack, J. P., D. T. Jones, and D. Roos. (1990a). "How Lean Production Can Change the World. *The Business World*, pp. 21–38.

———. (1990b). *The Machine That Changed the World*. New York: Macmillan.

Woodruff, D. (1992). "Detroit's Big Chance." *Business Week* (June 29), pp. 82–90.

"Workout." (1989). *GE Silicones News* (Dec.), Special ed., p. 1.

"Workout." (1991). *GE Silicones News* (Sept.), Special ed., pp. 1–2.

Young, J. (1990). "An American Giant Rethinks Globalization." *Information Strategy* (spring), pp. 5–10.

ABOUT THE AUTHORS

Yanan Ju is Professor of Communication at Central Connecticut State University. He earned his Ph.D. in political science from the University of Belgrade. Ju has taught at China's Fudan University, University of Connecticut, and University of North Carolina at Chapel Hill. Ju has authored/coauthored or edited/coedited a dozen books and numerous articles in both English and Chinese. His most recent publication is *The Great Wall in Ruins, Communication and Cultural Change in China* (coauthored with Godwin Chu), also from SUNY Press.

Donald P. Cushman is Professor of Communication at the State University of New York at Albany. Cushman earned his Ph.D. in communiction from the University of Wisconsin–Madison. He has also taught at Michigan State University and University of California–Santa Barbara. An author/coauthor or editor/coeditor of a dozen books and numerous articles, Cushman has been a pioneer scholar in high-speed management. His knowledge and experiences in the field have sent him around the world consulting for both private companies and government organizations.

INDEX

Adaptive organization, 96-98
Baldridge award, 48–49
Benchmarking, 4, 35, 40–55
   candidates, 50–52
   critical success factors, 54–55
   customer benchmarking, 43–44
   internal benchmarking, 47
   process of, 45
   process benchmarking, 42–44
   research on, 46
   strategic benchmarking, 41–42, 44
Business climate, 16–17

Coalignment, 116–119
   studies on, 118–119
Communication, 1
   communication technologies, 13–14
Competitive advantage, 16, 25–26, 123–131
Continuous improvement program, 3

DLM (Distributed leadership model), 66

Economic development model, 15
Environmental scanning, 21–24, 31–32, 103–105, 120–123

GE (General Electric), 78–81

High-speed management, 11, 31–32, 102–103
   assumptions of, 17–20
   data, 29–30
   emergence of, 12–13
   theory of, 21

International competition, 24–25

Just-in-time, 74

Organizational structure, 85–100
   hierarchy, 89–91

Speed-to-market, 35–40, 103–104

Team, 3
   assessment, 8–9
   benchmarking team, 4
   composition, 39–40
   cross-functional team, 3
   culture, 91–93
   executive team, 4,
   leadership patterns, 6–7
   outside linking team, 4,
   self-managed team, 3
   superior work team, 61–62
   synergy, 3
Team embeddedness (or anchorage), 5, 101–114
   cultural anchorage, 109–111

Team embedeness *(continued)*
  dynamic nature of, 113–114
  psychological embededness, 5, 111–112
  skills embededness, 5, 112–113
  social embededness, 5
  structural anchorage, 106–109
  task embededness, 5
Teamwork, 1, 33–34, 85, 133–138
  at GE, 78–81
  at Toyota, 78
  cross-functional teamwork, 62–64
  defining features of, 1, 57–73
  executive-level teamwork, 67–70
  model of, 81–83
  patterns of, 57–73
  self-managed teamwork, 64–67
  social-technical teamwork, 70–72
  studies on, 1, 4
Toyota, 73–77, 124–126

Value chain theory, 24, 26–28, 31–32, 105–106, 123–131
  application of, 28–31
Virtual organization, 98–100

Welch, Jack, 23–24, 78–81, 86
Work groups, 60–61